HOW TO DEAL WITH EMOTIONALLY IMMATURE PARENTS

HOW TO DEAL WITH EMOTIONALLY IMMATURE PARENTS

HEALING FROM NARCISSISTIC, AUTHORITARIAN, PERMISSIVE, ENMESHED, OR ABSENT PARENTS

GENERATIONAL HEALING
BOOK 2

ESSIE WOODARD

Book Bound
STUDIOS

To the brave souls who journey through the shadows of the past to bring light to the future—this book is dedicated to you. May the insights within these pages offer understanding, healing, and the courage to foster emotional maturity in ourselves and those we touch. Together, we can break the cycles of the past and build a legacy of emotional health for generations to come.

Emotional growth is the only really enduring growth there is.

— CARL R. ROGERS

CONTENTS

UNDERSTANDING EMOTIONAL IMMATURITY

The Landscape of Emotional Immaturity

In the realm of family dynamics, emotional immaturity in parents is a phenomenon that, while often unspoken, casts long shadows across their children's lives. It is a landscape marked by behaviors and attitudes that, at their core, reveal a stunted development in emotional regulation, empathy, and self-awareness. These parents may not necessarily lack love or good intentions for their children. Still, their emotional responses can be unpredictable, self-centered, or childish, leading to a confusing and sometimes painful upbringing.

It is essential to recognize the various contours that define emotional immaturity to navigate this landscape. These parents may exhibit a limited emotional vocabulary, often struggling to articulate their feelings or understand the emotional cues of others. Their reactions to stress can be impulsive, and they might prioritize their emotional needs over those of their children. This can manifest in dismissive, intrusive, or even neglectful behaviors, depending on the situation at hand.

A lack of consistent nurturing and support often characterizes the emotional climate created by such parents. Children in these environments might find themselves playing the caretaker role as they learn to manage their own emotions and those of their parents. This role reversal can lead to an accelerated loss of childhood innocence as children are compelled to navigate adult emotions and responsibilities prematurely.

Moreover, emotionally immature parents may struggle with boundaries, either being overly enmeshed with their children or, conversely, detached and uninvolved. This inconsistency can leave children feeling insecure and unsure about their place in the family and the world. They might grapple with guilt for desiring independence or harbor resentment for the emotional labor they've been shouldered.

Understanding the landscape of emotional immaturity in parents is crucial in recognizing the patterns and impacts of such upbringing. It is a terrain that requires careful navigation, for the echoes of childhood experiences can resonate well into adulthood. As we delve deeper into the nuances of emotional immaturity, we can unravel the complex tapestry of behaviors and motivations that shape these parental relationships, paving the way for healing and growth for both parents and their children.

Defining Emotional Immaturity in Parents

Emotional maturity refers to the ability to manage and understand one's emotions, engage with others in empathetic and considerate ways, and navigate relationships' complexities with a sense of responsibility and foresight. Conversely, emotional immaturity in parents manifests as a chronic pattern of emotional responses that are more aligned with those of a much younger individual, often marked by impulsivity, self-centeredness, and a limited capacity for empathy.

Emotionally immature parents may struggle to provide the emotional support and stability that children require for healthy development. This immaturity does not necessarily stem from a lack of love or concern for their offspring. Instead, it is indicative of an underdeveloped emotional skill set. These parents may have difficulty processing their own emotions maturely, which can lead to a range of challenging behaviors for both themselves and their children.

One of the hallmarks of emotional immaturity is a tendency to prioritize one's needs and feelings over those of others. In the context of parenting, this can translate into a lack of attunement to a child's emotional needs. An emotionally immature parent may react to their child's expressions of feelings with dismissal, irritation, or even mockery. Such responses can leave children feeling misunderstood and unsupported and may instill a sense of emotional isolation.

Another characteristic of emotional immaturity is poor emotional regulation. Parents who have not developed this skill may exhibit mood swings, explosive anger, or passive-aggressive behavior. These unpredictable emotional responses can create an environment of instability and anxiety for children, who thrive on consistency and predictability from their caregivers.

Furthermore, emotionally immature parents may struggle with boundaries, either being overly rigid and authoritarian or, conversely, too permissive, failing to set appropriate limits for behavior. This inconsistency can confuse children who benefit from clear and consistent guidelines. Without these, children may struggle to develop self-discipline and an understanding of acceptable social behavior.

It is also worth noting that emotional immaturity is not always constant. Parents may exhibit mature emotional responses in certain situations while reverting to immature patterns in others. This inconsistency can be particularly disorienting for children, who may find it difficult to predict how their parents will react at any given time.

Understanding the nature of emotional immaturity in parents is the first step toward addressing its effects within the family unit. It is a complex issue requiring compassion and insight to navigate successfully. As we delve deeper into the impact of emotional immaturity on family dynamics in the following discussions, we will explore the challenges it presents and the pathways to growth and healing for both parents and children.

The Impact on Family Dynamics

The impact of emotionally immature parents on family dynamics is profound and multifaceted. Children raised in such environments often find themselves in the paradoxical position of having to navigate the unpredictable emotional landscapes of their caregivers while simultaneously striving to develop their sense of stability and self-worth.

One of the most significant consequences is the role reversal that can occur within the family structure. Children may find themselves stepping into the caretaker role, providing emotional support, or managing household responsibilities beyond their years. This premature thrust into adult-like duties can lead to losing childhood innocence and the necessary space to explore and understand their emotions and needs.

Moreover, the emotional development of these children can be stunted as they mirror the immature emotional responses they observe. They may struggle with expressing their feelings appropriately or understanding the emotional cues of others, which can lead to difficulties in forming healthy relationships outside the family unit.

The communication patterns within a family headed by emotionally immature parents can also be significantly affected. Such parents may avoid open discussions about feelings, preferring to sweep issues under the rug or react with volatility rather than engage in constructive dialogue. This can create an environment where children feel unheard and invalidated, fostering a sense of isolation and confusion about effectively communicating their thoughts and emotions.

Furthermore, the unpredictability of an emotionally immature parent's reactions can instill a sense of chronic anxiety in children. They may walk on eggshells, constantly vigilant and trying to anticipate their parents' mood swings or irrational behavior. This hyper-awareness can lead to excessive stress and an inability to relax and feel safe within the home environment.

The emotional climate set by immature parents often lacks consistency, which is essential for children to develop a secure attachment style. Without the assurance of a stable, nurturing environment, children may develop insecure or disorganized attachment patterns, affecting their ability to trust and connect with others throughout their lives.

In essence, the impact of emotionally immature parents on family dynamics extends far beyond the immediate family interactions. It can influence children's psychological and emotional well-being long into adulthood, shaping how they perceive themselves, engage with others, and form their own relationships. Within this understanding, we can begin to appreciate the importance of recognizing the signs of emotional immaturity in parents, not only for the benefit of the children involved but for the health of the family unit as a whole.

Recognizing the Signs

In comprehending the complexities of emotional immaturity in parents, it is essential to identify the hallmarks that characterize such behavior. Emotional immaturity can manifest in various ways, often subtle and interwoven into daily interactions, making them challenging to discern. Yet, recognizing these signs is a critical step towards understanding and addressing the issues that arise from being raised by emotionally immature parents.

One of the most telling signs is inconsistency in emotional responses. Emotionally immature parents may react unpredictably to their child's needs or emotions. They might respond with empathy and support one moment, only to be dismissive or even hostile the next. This unpredictability can create a sense of instability and insecurity in children, who learn to tread carefully in the emotional landscape of their home, never quite sure which version of their parent they will encounter.

Another indicator is a tendency towards self-centeredness. Parents with emotional immaturity may prioritize their feelings and needs over their children's. They might seek attention and validation from their child, reversing the typical parent-child dynamic. This self-focus can prevent them from being fully present and attentive to their child's experiences, often leading to a lack of emotional support when the child needs it most.

Difficulty in handling stress and conflict is also a common trait among emotionally immature parents. Instead of approaching challenges with resilience and problem-solving skills, they may become overwhelmed or avoidant. This inability to cope effectively with the everyday stresses of life can leave children feeling alone in navigating their difficulties, as they cannot rely on their parents for guidance or support.

Emotionally immature parents may also struggle with boundaries. They might overshare personal problems or treat their child as a confidant, burdening them with issues that are inappropriate for their age. Conversely, they may be invasive, not respecting their child's privacy or autonomy, hindering their healthy sense of self-development.

Lastly, more emotional depth is often needed. These parents may struggle to engage in deep, meaningful conversations about feelings, dreams, or fears. Their interactions might remain superficial, focused on day-to-day tasks or small talk, leaving their child hungry for a more profound connection that remains unmet.

Recognizing these signs is not about casting blame but gaining insight into the relational patterns that may have shaped one's upbringing. It is the first step in a compassionate journey toward understanding and healing. As we move forward, we will explore how this newfound understanding can set the stage for personal growth and healthier relationships, not just with one's parents but in all areas of life.

Setting the Stage for Healing and Growth

In the journey of understanding our parents and the impact of their emotional immaturity on our lives, recognition is merely the first step. It is akin to turning on a light in a dimly lit room, allowing us to see the contours of the furniture that we've been stumbling over for years. But once we see the obstacles, the question arises: what do we do next? How do we navigate this newfound awareness towards healing and growth?

The process of healing is not linear, nor is it one-size-fits-all. It requires patience, self-compassion, and, often, a reevaluation of the narratives we've held about ourselves and our familial relationships. To set the stage for healing and growth, we must first establish a foundation of understanding—not just our parents' limitations but also our responses.

One of the most profound realizations that can come from recognizing emotional immaturity in parents is the recognition of our survival strategies. As children, we adapt to our environment in ways that allow us to cope with unpredictability and emotional neglect. These adaptations can manifest as hyper-independence, people-pleasing, or an overdeveloped sense of responsibility for others' emotions. While these strategies may have served us in our youth, they can become maladaptive in adulthood, leading to behavior patterns that no longer serve our best interests.

To move forward, it is essential to cultivate an inner dialogue that is both kind and truthful. This means acknowledging the pain and disappointment that come with having emotionally immature parents while also recognizing that we have the power to rewrite our own story. It involves grieving the loss of the parent-child dynamic we may have longed for and, in its place, building an autonomous and resilient sense of self.

Self-care becomes a critical component in setting this stage. It is about creating boundaries that protect our emotional well-being, engaging in activities that nourish us, and seeking out reciprocal and grounding relationships. It is also about learning to parent ourselves in the ways we needed but did not receive. This might include developing emotional regulation skills, practicing self-compassion, and pursuing personal goals that align with our values and aspirations.

Moreover, setting the stage for healing and growth often involves seeking external support. This could come through therapy, support groups, or educational resources that provide insight and validation. It is essential to surround ourselves with individuals who understand the nuanced challenges of having emotionally immature parents and who can offer empathy and guidance as we navigate this complex terrain.

As we embark on this path, it is crucial to remember that healing is not about changing our parents or expecting them to become the figures we need them to be. It is about changing our relationship to our past, taking control of our narrative, and stepping into a future where our emotional well-being is no longer contingent on our capacity for growth.

In this process, we may discover strengths we never knew we had and a capacity for forgiveness and understanding that does not excuse harmful behavior but transcends it. We are not erasing the past by setting the stage for healing and growth. Still, instead, we are permitting ourselves to emerge from its shadow, grow beyond the confines of our upbringing, and cultivate a life rich with emotional maturity and fulfillment.

1

THE ORIGINS OF EMOTIONAL IMMATURITY

Generational Patterns and Legacy

Emotional immaturity in parents is a complex phenomenon that often does not arise in isolation. As we delve into the intricate tapestry of family dynamics, it becomes evident that the roots of such immaturity can frequently be traced back through generations. This legacy of emotional underdevelopment is not merely a repetition of behaviors but a continuation of unaddressed emotional needs and unresolved psychological conflicts.

To understand the generational patterns that contribute to emotional immaturity, it is essential to recognize the role of the family environment in shaping an individual's emotional landscape. Children observe and internalize the emotional responses and coping mechanisms of their caregivers. When parents exhibit emotionally immature behaviors—such as difficulty in handling stress, poor communication skills, or an inability to empathize with others—these traits can become the blueprint for their children's emotional development.

In many cases, emotionally immature parents may have experienced similar deficiencies in their upbringing. Perhaps they were raised in households where emotional expression was discouraged or even punished, suppressing their emotional growth. In such environments, emotions are often viewed as a source of weakness or inconvenience rather than a natural and healthy part of the human experience.

This suppression can create a cycle where emotional expression and healthy emotional regulation are not modeled or taught, leaving children ill-equipped to manage their emotions effectively. As these children grow into adults and become parents themselves, they may struggle with the same emotional limitations that their parents did, perpetuating the cycle.

Moreover, societal and cultural factors can also significantly influence this generational legacy. In some cultures, for example, stoicism is highly valued, and emotional vulnerability is seen as undesirable. Such cultural norms can reinforce the cycle of emotional immaturity, as individuals may feel pressured to conform to these expectations, even when it is detrimental to their emotional well-being.

The impact of historical events on emotional development is also worth considering. Families that have endured trauma, such as war, displacement, or severe economic hardship, may carry the emotional scars of these experiences across generations. The survival mechanisms developed during times of crisis can become ingrained, with emotional openness and vulnerability being sidelined in favor of resilience and self-reliance.

Despite these patterns, it is essential to remember that generational legacies of emotional immaturity are not inescapable destinies. With awareness and effort, individuals can break the cycle. By seeking to understand their emotional heritage and actively working to develop healthier emotional skills, parents can create a new legacy—one that is characterized by emotional maturity and the capacity for deeper, more fulfilling relationships with their children and others.

In recognizing these patterns and their origins, we pave the way for a more compassionate understanding of emotionally immature parents. This understanding is not an excuse for their behaviors but rather a context that can inform the journey toward healing and growth. As we move forward, we will explore the psychological theories that provide further insight into the mechanisms behind emotional immaturity, shedding light on the internal workings of the emotionally underdeveloped mind.

Psychological Theories Behind Emotional Immaturity

In exploring the origins of emotional immaturity in parents, it is essential to delve into the psychological theories that provide a framework for understanding this complex phenomenon. Emotional immaturity can manifest in various behaviors, such as difficulty handling emotions, poor empathy, and a tendency to react rather than respond to challenging situations. These behaviors affect the parents and have profound implications for their children's emotional development.

One of the foundational theories in psychology that sheds light on emotional immaturity is Sigmund Freud's psychoanalytic theory, particularly his concept of the id, ego, and superego. According to Freud, the id is the primitive and instinctual part of the mind that contains sexual and aggressive drives and hidden memories. The superego operates as a moral conscience, and the ego is the realistic part that mediates between the desires of the id and the superego. In the case of emotionally immature parents, there may be an imbalance in these psychic structures, often with a dominant id that drives impulsive, child-like behavior and an underdeveloped superego that fails to temper these impulses with mature moral reasoning.

Another significant theory is Erik Erikson's stages of psychosocial development, which suggests that emotional maturity results from successfully navigating a series of life stages, each with its unique challenge and potential for growth. For some parents, emotional immaturity may stem from difficulties in their developmental stages, resulting in a lack of essential skills such as trust, autonomy, and initiative. These unresolved issues can lead to stagnation and an inability to provide the emotional support and guidance their children need.

Behaviorism, as proposed by John B. Watson and further developed by B.F. Skinner also offers insights into emotional immaturity. This perspective focuses on observable behaviors and how they are learned through interaction with the environment. Emotionally immature parents may have learned maladaptive emotional responses through their experiences and reinforcement histories. They might not have had positive role models to emulate or may have been rewarded for immature behaviors, perpetuating a cycle of emotional underdevelopment.

Cognitive theories, particularly those of Jean Piaget, emphasize the role of mental processes in understanding the world. Piaget's stages of cognitive development highlight how individuals construct a mental model of the world at different ages. Suppose a parent's cognitive development is arrested at a particular stage, perhaps due to trauma or lack of educational opportunities. In that case, they may struggle with abstract thinking or perspective-taking, which is crucial for mature emotional interactions.

Lastly, the humanistic perspective, championed by psychologists such as Carl Rogers and Abraham Maslow, focuses on the individual's capacity for growth and self-actualization. Emotional immaturity in parents might be viewed through this lens as a failure to reach one's potential for psychological growth, often due to conditions not conducive to fostering self-awareness and personal development. These parents may have grown up in environments that did not value or support the exploration of personal emotions and needs, leading to stunted emotional growth.

Understanding these psychological theories provides a backdrop against which we can better comprehend the intricacies of emotional immaturity in parents. It is not a singular issue with a one-size-fits-all explanation but a tapestry woven from various psychological influences and life experiences. As we unravel this tapestry, we will consider how attachment styles, formed early in life, play a pivotal role in shaping the emotional maturity of parents.

The Role of Attachment Styles

Understanding the origins of emotional immaturity in parents often requires us to delve into the complex world of attachment styles. Attachment theory, first developed by John Bowlby and later expanded by Mary Ainsworth, provides a framework for understanding how the bonds formed between children and their caregivers can influence emotional development and behavior later in life.

Attachment styles are bonding patterns that can affect how individuals relate to others, including their own children. These styles are typically categorized as secure, anxious-preoccupied, dismissive-avoidant, and fearful-avoidant. A healthy balance of intimacy and independence characterizes secure attachment. In contrast, the other three styles, known as insecure attachments, can lead to various emotional challenges.

When parents have an insecure attachment style, they may struggle with emotional regulation and interpersonal relationships. For instance, a parent with an anxious-preoccupied attachment may become overly dependent on their child for emotional support, leading to a dynamic where the child feels responsible for the parent's emotional well-being. Conversely, a dismissive-avoidant parent may be emotionally distant, making it difficult for the child to form a close, nurturing bond.

These insecure attachment styles can stem from the parent's own childhood experiences. Suppose they did not receive consistent care and emotional support from their caregivers. In that case, they might not have developed the skills to nurture a secure attachment with their children. This lack of secure attachment can manifest as emotional immaturity, where the parent may be unable to provide the empathy, stability, and responsiveness that their child needs.

Intergenerational patterns can also perpetuate emotional immaturity in parents. Suppose emotionally immature caregivers raised a parent. In that case, they might inadvertently replicate the same behaviors with their children, not because of a conscious choice but because it is the only parenting model they know.

It is essential to recognize that attachment styles are not static and can change over time with self-awareness and effort. Parents who identify with an insecure attachment style can seek therapy and support to develop healthier ways of relating to their children. By doing so, they can break the cycle of emotional immaturity and foster a more secure and nurturing environment for their family.

As we move forward, it is crucial to consider the psychological underpinnings of emotional immaturity and the broader societal and cultural contexts that shape parenting practices. These external influences can either exacerbate the challenges faced by emotionally immature parents or provide avenues for support and growth.

Societal and Cultural Influences

In exploring the origins of emotional immaturity in parents, it is essential to consider the broader societal and cultural influences that shape individual behaviors and attitudes. While the attachment styles discussed earlier play a significant role in the development of emotional maturity, the environment in which a person is raised and continues to live can exert a powerful influence on their emotional development.

Society and culture are invisible forces dictating norms, values, and expectations. These forces can either support emotional growth or stifle it. In many cultures, there is an emphasis on maintaining social harmony and overexpressing individual emotions, which can lead to adults who are adept at keeping the peace but need to be more skilled at recognizing and managing their feelings or those of their children. This can result in a form of emotional neglect, where parents may provide for the physical needs of their children but remain disconnected from their emotional needs.

Furthermore, certain cultural narratives glorify self-sacrifice and the suppression of personal needs for the sake of family or community. Parents who internalize these values may struggle to model healthy emotional boundaries for their children. They might prioritize the external appearance of a well-functioning family while neglecting the emotional dialogues that foster intimacy and understanding.

In addition to cultural narratives, societal structures and pressures contribute to emotional immaturity. The relentless pace of modern life, the emphasis on material success, and the often unattainable standards of perfection can leave parents feeling inadequate and overwhelmed. This chronic stress can impede their ability to be present and emotionally responsive to their children. When parents are preoccupied with the demands of work and the pursuit of status, they may inadvertently model a disconnection from their inner emotional world.

Moreover, the rise of digital technology and social media has created a new landscape for parental emotional immaturity. The constant bombardment of curated images of 'perfect' families and parenting can create unrealistic expectations and a sense of failure. Parents may focus more on projecting an ideal image than engaging in the messy, authentic emotional exchanges that genuine relationships require.

It is also essential to recognize the intergenerational transmission of emotional patterns. Parents who are emotionally immature caregivers may not have had the opportunity to learn healthy emotional regulation and expression. Without conscious effort and support, these patterns can be passed down, perpetuating a cycle of emotional disconnect.

Understanding the societal and cultural influences on emotional immaturity is not about assigning blame but gaining insight into the complex web of factors contributing to this issue. By recognizing these influences, parents and those who support them can begin to identify the changes needed to foster emotional growth and maturity, both for themselves and for the next generation.

As we move forward, it becomes clear that while societal and cultural influences are significant, they are not the only factors at play. Individual experiences, particularly those involving trauma, can have a profound impact on emotional development. Addressing these personal histories is crucial in breaking the cycle of emotional immaturity.

Trauma and Its Aftermath

Trauma can be a chisel that shapes the psyche in profound and often unsettling ways. When considering the development of emotional immaturity in parents, it is essential to explore the role that traumatic experiences may play in this dynamic. Trauma, particularly when experienced during one's formative years, can arrest emotional development, leading to behaviors and patterns that persist into adulthood and parenthood.

In the wake of trauma, individuals often adopt coping mechanisms that can be maladaptive. While initially serving as a means of psychological survival, these mechanisms can become entrenched and manifest as emotional immaturity. For instance, a parent who experienced abandonment as a child might struggle with emotional availability, fearing that closeness will inevitably lead to loss. Alternatively, a parent who endured emotional abuse may find it challenging to engage in healthy communication, perhaps resorting to sarcasm or withdrawal in times of stress.

The aftermath of trauma can also lead to a preoccupation with control, as unpredictability may feel intolerable to someone whose past was marked by chaotic or harmful experiences. This need for control can stifle the spontaneity and openness required for nurturing parent-child relationships. It can also lead to rigidity in thinking and behavior, making it difficult for such parents to adapt to the evolving needs of their children or to model emotional resilience.

Moreover, trauma can impair a person's ability to self-regulate emotions. Parents who have not had the opportunity or support to process their traumatic experiences may be prone to emotional outbursts or, conversely, emotional numbness. Both extremes create an environment where children may struggle to learn healthy emotional regulation themselves.

It is essential to recognize that trauma does not destine one to become an emotionally immature parent. Many individuals demonstrate remarkable resilience and, with support and healing, can break the cycle of trauma to become emotionally attuned caregivers. However, without addressing the wounds of the past, the likelihood of perpetuating patterns of emotional immaturity increases.

Compassion is a critical component in addressing the intergenerational impact of trauma. By understanding the origins of a parent's emotional struggles, families can begin to foster an environment of healing and growth. This often involves professional support, such as therapy, which can provide the tools and space for individuals to work through their traumatic experiences and develop healthier emotional habits.

In this context, it is crucial to approach the subject of emotionally immature parents not with judgment but with an empathetic understanding of the complex interplay between past trauma and present behavior. By doing so, we can open pathways to healing and transformation that benefit the parents and their children and the familial legacy they will leave behind.

Chapter Summary

- Emotional immaturity in parents often stems from generational patterns and unresolved psychological conflicts.
- Children learn emotional responses from their parents, which can affect their emotional development if they are immature.
- Cultural norms and societal expectations can reinforce emotional immaturity by discouraging emotional expression.
- Historical traumas experienced by families can lead to emotional scars that affect future generations.
- Psychological theories like Freud's psychoanalytic theory and Erikson's stages of development help explain emotional immaturity.
- Attachment styles formed in childhood influence how parents relate to their children and can perpetuate emotional immaturity.

- Societal pressures and cultural narratives can contribute to emotional immaturity by emphasizing material success over emotional connection.
- Trauma, especially in early life, can arrest emotional development and lead to maladaptive coping mechanisms in parents.

2

PROFILES OF EMOTIONALLY
IMMATURE PARENTS

The Narcissistic Parent

In the landscape of emotionally immature parenting, the narcissistic parent often casts a long shadow, one that can shape the emotional terrain of a child's life in profound ways. An overarching self-interest and a deep need for admiration and validation characterize this type of parent. Their emotional immaturity is not marked by a lack of intelligence or love but rather by a self-centered approach to relationships that can leave their children feeling secondary to their parent's desires and image.

The narcissistic parent may present a polished and charming façade to the outside world, often appearing confident and accomplished. To their children, however, they can be unpredictable and sometimes cruel, as their need for control and adoration takes precedence over the child's needs for support and autonomy. It is not uncommon for these parents to have high expectations of their children, not necessarily for the child's benefit, but as a reflection of their image. Children may feel pressured to perform or conform to their parent's idealized vision, leading to a sense of inadequacy and a lack of genuine self-esteem.

One of the hallmarks of the narcissistic parent is their inability to empathize with their child. They struggle to recognize and respond to their child's feelings as separate from their own. When a child expresses needs or emotions that do not align with the parent's self-image or agenda, the parent may react with indifference, irritation, or hostility. This lack of attunement can lead to a child doubting their feelings and experiences, often carrying into adulthood a tendency to dismiss their emotional needs.

The relationship dynamics with a narcissistic parent can be particularly challenging because the parent may use affection and approval as tools for manipulation. Love and attention may be given conditionally, withdrawn as a form of punishment, or used to coax the child into compliance. This inconsistency can create an anxious attachment in the child, who learns to be hyper-vigilant to the parent's moods and prioritize their emotional state over their own.

Despite these challenges, it is essential to recognize that the child of a narcissistic parent can learn to navigate this complex relationship and develop a strong sense of self. With support, understanding, and perhaps therapeutic intervention, individuals can work through the confusion and hurt that may come from being raised by a narcissistic parent. They can learn to set boundaries, cultivate self-compassion, and build healthy relationships that affirm their worth and autonomy.

As we continue to explore the profiles of emotionally immature parents, it becomes clear that each type presents unique challenges and opportunities for growth. Understanding these profiles helps us empathize with those who have been shaped by such relationships and empowers us to break cycles of emotional immaturity for future generations.

The Authoritarian Parent

The authoritarian parent stands as a figure of unwavering control and rigid expectations. Unlike the narcissistic parent, whose self-absorption can lead to a volatile and unpredictable environment, the authoritarian parent creates a world with clearly defined rules and roles, leaving little room for flexibility or open dialogue.

The authoritarian parent's approach to child-rearing is characterized by a strict adherence to discipline and a focus on obedience. They often believe that children should be seen and not heard and that questioning parental authority is tantamount to disrespect. This type of parent values order and tradition, and they often rely on the phrase "because I said so" as a final word to shut down any form of negotiation or protest.

Children raised by authoritarian parents may learn to follow the rules well. Still, they often do so at the expense of their self-expression and autonomy. The fear of punishment or disapproval can lead these children to become excellent rule-followers. Still, they may struggle with self-esteem and the ability to think independently. They may also associate love and acceptance with performance and compliance, which can carry into their adult relationships and self-perception.

The emotional immaturity of the authoritarian parent is evident in their inability to empathize with their children's feelings and needs. They focus on maintaining control rather than fostering an environment where children can safely express emotions and learn through trial and error. This can result in a disconnect between parent and child, where the child feels that their emotional world is neither understood nor valued.

It is essential to recognize that the authoritarian parent's behavior often stems from their upbringing or a deep-seated fear of chaos and disorder. They may equate control with care and believe that by enforcing strict rules, they are preparing their children for the world's harsh realities. However, this can inadvertently stifle a child's development of critical life skills such as problem-solving, negotiation, and emotional regulation.

In contrast to the authoritarian parent's rigidity, other parenting styles offer a more balanced approach, where structure is present but not suffocating and where children are encouraged to develop a sense of self within safe boundaries. As we continue to explore the various profiles of emotionally immature parents, it becomes increasingly clear that the emotional health of a parent plays a pivotal role in the emotional development of their children. The key lies in finding a balance that nurtures discipline and dialogue, allowing children to grow into emotionally mature and resilient adults.

The Permissive Parent

The permissive parent often stands in stark contrast to the authoritarian figure we have previously explored. Where the authoritarian imposes rigid boundaries and high expectations, the permissive parent is characterized by a notable lack of them. This type of parent may appear more as a friend than a guardian, often driven by an aversion to conflict and a deep-seated desire to be liked by their children.

An indulgent attitude typically marks the permissive parent's approach. They may allow their children to set their schedules, make their own decisions, and face few consequences for misbehavior. This laissez-faire style is not born of a lack of love or concern; rather, it often stems from the parent's own emotional needs and insecurities. They may feel incapable of setting and enforcing rules or fear that by doing so, they will push their children away.

While this might create a household with a seemingly relaxed atmosphere, the long-term effects on children can be profound. With clear boundaries and consistent guidance, children may be able to develop self-discipline and an understanding of appropriate behavior.

They may also form an unrealistic view of the world, one in which their actions do not have significant consequences, which can lead to challenges in their adult lives, particularly in professional environments or personal relationships where structure and accountability are essential.

The permissive parent's emotional immaturity is often reflected in their inability to tolerate the everyday stresses of parenting. They may seek to avoid the discomfort of being the 'bad guy' and thus shirk the responsibility of disciplining their children. This avoidance can be deeply rooted in their own experiences of being parented, perhaps mirroring the permissive or neglectful styles they were subjected to.

Children of permissive parents may also find themselves feeling a sense of emptiness or lack of direction. While they may not have experienced the overt control of an authoritarian parent, they lack the secure framework to test their limits and learn from their mistakes. As these children grow, they may seek out or create structure in other areas of their lives to compensate for what was missing in their upbringing.

It is essential to recognize that permissive parenting, like other styles, is often an unconscious replication of the parent's emotional world. Compassion for the parent and the child is crucial in understanding this dynamic. The permissive parent is not without love or good intentions; they are often unequipped to provide the structure and consistent guidance that is a cornerstone of mature parenting.

As we move forward in our exploration of emotionally immature parents, we will encounter the enmeshed parent whose intense involvement in their child's life presents a different set of challenges and impacts on the child's development. Understanding the nuances of each parenting style allows us to see the spectrum of emotional immaturity and its diverse manifestations within family dynamics.

The Enmeshed Parent

The enmeshed parent presents a unique set of challenges and characteristics that can profoundly affect the family dynamic. Unlike the permissive parent, who may take a more hands-off approach, the enmeshed parent is excessively involved and often oversteps personal boundaries, leading to an intricately intertwined relationship with their child to the point where individual identities seem blurred.

The enmeshed parent often sees no distinction between their emotional needs and their child's. They may rely on their child for support, companionship, and even emotional stability, placing an undue burden on the child's shoulders. This can manifest in various ways, from the parent sharing inappropriate personal details and treating the child as a confidant to expecting the child to fulfill emotional roles typically reserved for an adult partner.

This dynamic can lead to several developmental issues for the child. As they grow, these children may struggle with forming a sense of self, as their needs and emotions have been deeply entangled with their parents. They may have difficulty recognizing where their parent's feelings end and begin, which can lead to challenges in establishing healthy relationships outside the family unit.

The enmeshed parent's inability to recognize and respect boundaries often stems from their emotional immaturity. They may have an intense fear of abandonment or loneliness, which drives them to cling to their child. This can create a suffocating environment for the child, who may feel responsible for the parent's emotional well-being in the absence of appropriate boundaries.

Children of enmeshed parents may also exhibit high loyalty and devotion to their parents, often at the expense of their own needs and desires. This loyalty is not born out of a healthy, reciprocal relationship but out of a sense of obligation and the fear of what might happen if they do not meet their parent's emotional demands.

As these children transition into adulthood, they may encounter a host of issues, such as codependency in relationships, difficulty with decision-making, and a pervasive sense of guilt when asserting independence. While often rooted in the parent's deep love for their child, the enmeshed relationship can inadvertently stifle the child's growth into a fully autonomous individual.

It is crucial for those who have grown up with an enmeshed parent to recognize that their intense entanglement is not the blueprint for all relationships. Healing and growth come with understanding the dynamics of enmeshment and learning to establish healthy boundaries. This process often involves redefining one's sense of self apart from the parent and engaging in self-exploration and personal development.

For parents who identify with enmeshment tendencies, it is equally important to seek help understanding the origins of their behaviors and to learn how to foster a supportive yet independent relationship with their children. Through this, they can encourage their children's individuality and autonomy, essential for their emotional and psychological well-being.

In the broader context of emotionally immature parenting, the enmeshed parent represents a pattern where love and care, though undoubtedly present, are expressed in ways that can hinder rather than nurture. Through compassionate self-awareness and a commitment to change, parents and children can navigate the complexities of enmeshment and move towards healthier, more fulfilling relationships.

The Absent Parent

In the landscape of familial relationships, the figure of the absent parent is a stark contrast to the enmeshed parent we discussed earlier. Emotionally immature parents can manifest in various forms, and the absent parent is characterized by a pervasive detachment from their child's emotional world. This detachment is not necessarily physical; an absent parent can be present in the home but emotionally distant, creating an environment where a child may feel alone even in the company of family.

The absent parent often seems preoccupied with their own needs and interests, which can overshadow their child's emotional and sometimes even physical needs. This type of parent may avoid involvement in their child's life, not out of a lack of love but because they are overwhelmed by the demands of parenting or are simply ill-equipped to handle the emotional complexities of it. They may be seen as aloof or indifferent, and their interactions with their child can feel perfunctory or superficial.

Children of absent parents may struggle with feelings of abandonment. They may question their self-worth, wondering why they do not seem to merit their parent's attention or care. They might become excessively self-reliant, learning early on that they cannot depend on their parent for emotional support. This self-reliance can be a double-edged sword, fostering independence while reinforcing a deep-seated belief that they must go through life's challenges alone.

The emotional void left by an absent parent can lead to significant developmental impacts. A child may grow up with a skewed perception of relationships, believing emotional disconnection is typical. They may also need help recognizing or expressing their emotions, having never been taught or shown how to do so healthily.

Acknowledging that the absent parent is not always absent by choice is essential. Factors such as mental health issues, substance abuse, or a history of being raised by emotionally immature parents themselves can contribute to their detachment. Compassion for both the parent and child is crucial in understanding this dynamic. Healing can begin with recognizing the absent parent's limitations and the child's unmet emotional needs.

As we navigate through the complexities of emotionally immature parents, it becomes evident that the patterns established in childhood can profoundly influence one's emotional landscape into adulthood. The journey toward understanding and healing is a complex path. Still, with insight and support, individuals can learn to fill the gaps an absent parent leaves and build fulfilling emotional connections in their lives.

Chapter Summary

- The narcissistic parent prioritizes their own needs for admiration and control, often at the expense of their child's emotional well-being.
- Children of narcissistic parents may feel pressured to meet their parent's expectations and struggle with self-esteem and empathy.
- The authoritarian parent enforces strict discipline and obedience, often stifling a child's autonomy and self-expression.

- Children raised by authoritarian parents may become rule-followers with issues in self-esteem and independent thinking.
- The permissive parent avoids conflict and sets few boundaries, leading to children who may lack self-discipline and understanding of consequences.
- The enmeshed parent overly involves themselves in their child's life, blurring boundaries and hindering the child's development of a separate identity.
- The absent parent is emotionally detached, leaving children feeling abandoned and questioning their self-worth.
- Each emotionally immature parent presents unique challenges. Still, individuals can navigate these relationships and foster personal growth with support and understanding.

3

THE CHILD'S PERSPECTIVE

Growing Up with Emotional Neglect

In the tender landscape of childhood, where the soil of self is still being tilled, the presence of emotionally immature parents can cast long shadows over the growth of a young psyche. Emotional neglect, a silent arbiter of pain, often goes unnoticed by the world outside the family unit. Yet, its impact is deeply felt by those who endure it.

For children in such environments, the absence of emotional attunement from their caregivers can be as stark as the absence of food or warmth. These children may learn to walk on tiptoe around the moods and whims of their parents, internalizing a belief that their feelings are secondary or, worse, irrelevant. The lack of validation for their emotional experiences can lead to a profound sense of loneliness and a belief that they are inherently flawed.

Emotional neglect from an immature parent often means that the child's emotional needs are not met with consistency or understanding. A parent may be physically present but emotionally distant, unable to engage with the child's inner world. The child learns to mute their emotional responses and to become self-reliant in their inner emotional landscape because the external support is unpredictable or nonexistent.

While a testament to the child's resilience, this self-reliance comes at a cost. The child may grow up feeling disconnected from their emotions, struggling to identify and express them. They may become adept at reading the emotional cues of others yet find themselves at a loss when it comes to interpreting their feelings. The need for validation, for someone to acknowledge and affirm their emotional reality, can become a silent yearning. This quest shapes their interactions and relationships into adulthood.

As these children navigate the complexities of life, they often carry with them the weight of unvalidated emotions. The quest for validation is not merely a search for affirmation from others but a more profound journey towards self-acknowledgment and self-compassion. It is about learning to recognize the validity of one's emotions and experiences despite the lack of recognition from their primary caregivers.

The journey towards healing and self-validation is arduous but manageable. It involves peeling back the layers of self-protection, unlearning the patterns of emotional neglect, and building a relationship with oneself that is based on kindness, acceptance, and understanding. It is about finding one's voice and learning to trust that voice as a guide towards a more integrated and emotionally fulfilling life.

In the next steps of this journey, we will explore the paths individuals take in their quest for validation, understanding how they seek to fill the void left by their upbringing and how they can ultimately find the validation they need.

The Quest for Validation

In a child's heart, the yearning for a parent's approval and understanding is as natural as breathing. Children often embark on a silent, solitary quest for validation when the guardians of their world are emotionally immature. This quest can shape their identities and color their perceptions of self-worth for years.

For these children, validation is not merely a want; it is an unmet need, a puzzle piece missing from their emotional development. It is the acknowledgment they crave that their feelings are real, their experiences are legitimate, and their existence is significant. In the absence of this recognition from emotionally immature parents, children may question the validity of their emotions and experiences, leading to a deep-seated sense of invisibility.

The quest for validation in the eyes of a child living with emotional neglect is a journey fraught with confusion. They may wonder why their accomplishments, however grand or small, often go unnoticed or are met with indifference. They may internalize the lack of emotional response as a reflection of their worth, mistakenly believing they do not deserve attention or praise.

As they grow, these children may become adept at reading their parents' subtle cues and moods, adjusting their behavior in the hope of eliciting a positive response. They may become performers in their lives, playing roles they believe will garner the validation they deeply desire. Yet, the applause they seek is often absent, and the curtain falls on their efforts without the anticipated acclaim.

The emotional toll of this quest can manifest in various ways. Some children may become overachievers, relentlessly pushing themselves in academics, sports, or other activities as they chase the elusive approval of their parents. Others may withdraw, becoming quiet observers in their homes, convinced that their voices are not worthy of being heard.

Despite these challenges, the quest for validation is also a testament to the resilience of the human spirit. While marked by heartache, it is a journey that can lead to a profound understanding of self-reliance and inner strength. These children may learn to seek validation from within, to trust their own emotions and judgments, and to build a sense of self-worth that is not contingent on the unpredictable responses of emotionally immature parents.

As we delve deeper into the experiences of these children, we will explore the coping mechanisms and survival strategies they develop in response to their complex emotional environments. While necessary for navigating childhood, these adaptations can impact their adult lives, influencing their relationships, self-image, and how they parent their children.

In understanding the quest for validation, we open a window into the hearts of those who have navigated the turbulent waters of emotional neglect. Through this empathetic lens, we can begin to appreciate the full scope of their resilience and the depth of their desire to be seen, heard, and valued.

Coping Mechanisms and Survival Strategies

For many, the presence of emotionally immature parents can cast long shadows over the growth of a young psyche. In their innate resilience and adaptability, children often develop a repertoire of coping mechanisms and survival strategies to navigate the unpredictable terrain of their caregivers' emotional volatility.

One such coping mechanism is adopting a role that provides a sense of stability within the family dynamic. The child may become the 'caretaker,' shouldering responsibilities far beyond their years, or the 'peacemaker,' constantly diffusing tensions to maintain harmony. While offering a temporary haven of predictability, these roles can also stifle the child's authentic development, as they contort themselves into shapes that please their parents rather than explore their identities.

Another common strategy is emotional camouflage. Children learn to mask their true feelings, presenting a façade that aligns with their parents' expectations. This can manifest as a perpetual agreeableness, a suppression of negative emotions, or an exaggerated display of traits that garner approval. The cost of this masquerade is often a deep sense of loneliness and a disconnection from their emotional core.

Some children find solace in the world of imagination, creating rich inner lives that offer refuge from the emotional barrenness of their surroundings. This inner sanctuary can foster creativity and resilience. Still, it may also lead to a sense of alienation from the external world, as the child retreats further into their mental haven to escape the emotional neglect or unpredictability they face.

Intellectualization is another fortress to which a child might retreat. The child creates a buffer against the emotional chaos at home by focusing on logic, facts, and learning. This pursuit of knowledge can be empowering, but it may also serve as a barrier against the vulnerability of emotional connection, leaving the child adept at reasoning but hesitant in matters of the heart.

In some cases, children become hyper-vigilant, attuned to the slightest shifts in their parents' moods or behaviors. This heightened alertness can be protective, allowing the child to anticipate and navigate potential conflicts. However, it can also lead to chronic anxiety and an inability to relax, as the child remains perpetually on guard for the next emotional upheaval.

It is essential to recognize that these coping mechanisms and survival strategies, while adaptive in a challenging home environment, can have long-term implications. As these children grow into adulthood, they may find that the very behaviors that once protected them now hinder their ability to form healthy relationships, pursue their true passions, or allow themselves to be vulnerable and authentic.

The journey of healing and growth for those who have navigated childhood with emotionally immature parents involves a delicate unraveling of these ingrained patterns. It requires a compassionate self-exploration and the courage to face the pain that was once too overwhelming for a child to bear. It is a path of reclaiming oneself, piece by piece and learning to thrive beyond survival.

The Sibling Experience

Growing up with emotionally immature parents can be a solitary journey. Still, when siblings are part of the family dynamic, the experience takes on additional complexity. Siblings may become allies, adversaries, or strangers to one another, depending on how they navigate the unpredictable emotional landscape set by their parents.

In some cases, siblings bond over their shared challenges. They find solace in knowing someone else truly understands their parents' erratic moods and demands. These siblings often develop a secret language of glances and gestures, a silent communication that speaks volumes of their mutual support. They may protect each other from emotional outbursts and even take on parental roles, providing the care and guidance they are not receiving.

However, the strain of an emotionally volatile household can also drive siblings apart. Competition for the limited resources of parental attention and affection can foster resentment. An emotionally immature parent may, intentionally or not, set siblings against each other, comparing them or using one to control the other. This can lead to a dynamic where siblings feel pitted against one another, each struggling to carve out their own space and identity within the family.

In families where one child is designated as the "golden child" and another as the "scapegoat," the disparity in treatment can create deep rifts. The favored child may feel guilty for the special treatment they receive, or they may internalize the belief that they are more deserving. Conversely, the scapegoated child may harbor feelings of unworthiness and resentment. These roles can become entrenched, following the siblings into adulthood and affecting their relationships for years.

Sometimes, a sibling may take on the role of the caretaker or "parentified" child, especially if they are significantly older than their siblings. This responsibility can be a heavy burden, as they sacrifice their needs and childhood to provide stability and support. The parentified child may struggle with resentment and loss, even as they love their siblings deeply and feel proud of their ability to care for them.

The emotional neglect and inconsistency often accompanying immature parenting can also lead siblings to disengage. They may grow up feeling like strangers, each retreating into their worlds as a means of self-preservation. Without the tools or examples to build healthy relationships, they may find it challenging to connect in meaningful ways, even as they long for a deeper bond.

As these siblings mature and reflect on their upbringing, they may grapple with complex emotions. The shared history of navigating their parents' emotional immaturity can be both a source of connection and a barrier to it. Some may find that they can reach out to their siblings with greater understanding and compassion as they heal, forging new relationships built on mutual respect and shared growth.

Others may find that the gap needs to be narrower or the behavior patterns too profoundly ingrained to bridge the divide. In these instances, the journey may be individual healing, learning to find peace with the past, and building a sense of family and community in other areas of their lives.

The sibling experience in the context of emotionally immature parents is as varied as the individuals involved. Each sibling navigates the terrain with their map, shaped by their unique perceptions and responses to their family environment. The paths they take can lead to incredibly resilient bonds or to painfully deep divides. Understanding these dynamics is crucial for anyone seeking to heal from such a childhood and those seeking to support them.

Adulthood Reckonings

As we journey through the landscape of adulthood, the long shadows cast by emotionally immature parents often stretch far beyond the confines of childhood. For many, realizing a parent's emotional immaturity crystallizes not in the throes of adolescence but in the fullness of adult life. This reckoning, while deeply personal, is a shared experience among those who have navigated the unpredictable waters of a child-hood overshadowed by a parent's emotional limitations.

In this stage of life, the child-now-adult begins to piece together the mosaic of their upbringing, often with the clarity that distance and independence afford. It is a time when the fog of confusion lifts, and the patterns of emotional immaturity that characterized their parents' behavior become starkly apparent. The once inexplicable reactions, the absence of empathy, or the relentless self-centeredness of a parent are now understood as part and parcel of a broader, more troubling dynamic.

This dawning of understanding, however, is not without its pain. There is a profound sense of grief that accompanies the recognition of what was missed in one's formative years—a nurturing stability, a sense of security, or the unconditional support that every child deserves. The adult child might grapple with a sense of loss for the emotional connection that was never fully realized, and perhaps, a mourning for the parent they needed but did not have.

Yet, within this reckoning lies the growth potential. It is an opportunity to break the cycle of emotional immaturity. The adult child, through reflection and often with the support of therapy or self-help resources, can begin to cultivate the emotional skills they were not taught. They learn to set boundaries, articulate their needs, and seek out reciprocal and nurturing relationships. This process is not linear; it is fraught with the challenges of unlearning deeply ingrained behaviors and the temptation to fall back into familiar patterns.

For some, this period also prompts a reevaluation of the relationship with their emotionally immature parents. Decisions must be made about the nature of that relationship moving forward. Can there be a dialogue, an understanding, or is the distance necessary for self-preservation? These are not choices made lightly but require a compassionate yet firm resolve.

In navigating these waters, the adult child may also find solace and solidarity with their siblings, as discussed previously. The shared history can be a source of mutual support. Still, it can also reveal divergent paths of coping and understanding. Each sibling's journey is unique, and how they reconcile their childhood experiences with their adult lives can vary widely.

The reckoning of adulthood is a testament to the resilience of the human spirit. It is about reclaiming one's narrative and stepping into an identity not defined by a parent's emotional shortcomings. It is about learning to parent oneself to provide the love, patience, and encouragement everyone deserves. And in this journey, there is hope—not only for the individual but for the generations that follow, as the cycle of emotional immaturity is acknowledged, understood, and, with determination and heart, finally broken.

Chapter Summary

- Emotional neglect by immature parents can profoundly affect a child's development, leading to feelings of loneliness and a belief in their inherent flaws.
- Children with emotionally distant parents learn to suppress their emotions and become self-reliant, which can disconnect them from their feelings and hinder emotional expression.
- The quest for validation becomes a central theme in these children's lives as they seek acknowledgment of their emotional experiences from others and, ultimately, themselves.
- Coping mechanisms developed in childhood, such as adopting specific roles or emotional camouflage, can long-term affect adult relationships and self-image.
- Siblings in such families may become allies or adversaries, with their relationships affected by the competition for parental attention or by taking on parental roles themselves.
- In adulthood, individuals with emotionally immature parents often experience a reckoning as they gain clarity on their upbringing and work to break the cycle of emotional immaturity.

- Adult children may need to reevaluate their relationship with their parents, setting boundaries or seeking distance for self-preservation.
- The journey towards healing involves self-compassion, learning to validate one's emotions, and building healthier relationships and self-identity.

4

COMMUNICATION BREAKDOWNS AND BARRIERS

The Language of Emotional Immaturity

In navigating the complex dynamics of families with emotionally immature parents, we often encounter a peculiar dialect—a language of emotional immaturity that can perplex and frustrate those who yearn for genuine connection and understanding. This language, marked by its own set of rules and patterns, can create significant communication barriers between parents and children, and it is essential to recognize its features to foster better relationships and healing.

Emotionally immature parents may communicate indirectly, favoring hints and suggestions over clear and direct expression. This can leave their children in constant guesswork, trying to decipher the underlying messages or expectations. Such indirectness can stem from a parent's discomfort with vulnerability, fear of confrontation, or lack of awareness about effectively communicating.

Another characteristic of this language is minimization or trivialization, especially when faced with their child's emotions or needs. A parent might respond to a child's sadness or anger with comments like "Don't be so sensitive" or "It's not a big deal." This dismissive approach invalidates the child's experience and teaches them to doubt their own feelings and suppress their emotional expression.

Moreover, emotionally immature parents might resort to blame-shifting as a defense mechanism. When confronted with a mistake or a situation that requires accountability, they might deflect responsibility onto others, including their children. This can manifest in statements that imply the child is the cause of the parent's negative emotions or that the child's behavior is the sole problem, overlooking the parent's role in the dynamic.

Projection is another standard linguistic tool in the repertoire of emotionally immature communication. Parents may project their feelings, desires, or insecurities onto their children, accusing them of having motives or emotions that reflect the parent's internal world. This can be confusing and damaging to a child's sense of self as they struggle to separate their own identity from the distorted mirror their parent holds up to them.

Lastly, emotional immaturity can lead to a lack of consistency in communication. Parents may swing from being overly involved and controlling to being distant and disengaged, leaving their children unsure of where they stand. This inconsistency can create an unstable emotional environment where children must walk on eggshells, wondering which version of their parent they will encounter.

Understanding the language of emotional immaturity is crucial in breaking down the communication barriers in families with such dynamics. By recognizing these patterns, children of emotionally immature parents can begin to find their voice, establish boundaries, and seek healthier ways of relating both within and outside their family system. It is a journey that requires patience, self-compassion, and, often, the support of others who can provide the perspective and validation that emotionally immature parents may be unable to offer.

Avoidance and Denial

In the realm of family dynamics, the presence of emotionally immature parents can lead to a unique set of communication challenges. One of the most pervasive is the tendency toward avoidance and denial. This behavior can create an environment where open dialogue is stifled and emotional honesty is scarce.

In this context, avoidance manifests as an unwillingness to engage in conversations that might lead to emotional discomfort or require self-reflection. Emotionally immature parents may skillfully change the subject, make light of serious topics, or even physically remove themselves from situations that demand a more profound emotional engagement. This evasion is often not malicious but rather a profoundly ingrained defense mechanism. It is a way of preserving a self-image that may feel threatened by the vulnerability of such discussions.

On the other hand, denial is a more direct refusal to acknowledge the reality of a situation or the validity of another's feelings. When children, even adult children, attempt to express how certain behaviors have impacted them, emotionally immature parents may outright deny any wrongdoing or the emotional fallout of their actions. This denial can be particularly damaging as it invalidates the child's experiences and feelings, often leading to a sense of confusion and emotional isolation.

The interplay between avoidance and denial creates a barrier to authentic connection. Children of such parents may find themselves perpetually on the outskirts of genuine emotional intimacy, unable to penetrate the armor of avoidance and denial. This dynamic can leave children feeling unseen and unheard, with a gnawing sense that their emotional reality is neither acknowledged nor valued.

Understanding this pattern is crucial for those who find themselves in the shadow of emotionally immature parents. Recognizing avoidance and denial for what they are—defensive strategies rather than reflections of one's worth—can be the first step toward healing. It is also important to note that these behaviors are often deeply rooted in the parents' unresolved emotional issues, which they may be unconscious of or unwilling to confront.

For those navigating these waters, seeking out supportive relationships and environments where open and honest communication is possible and encouraged is essential. Establishing boundaries with parents who exhibit these behaviors can be challenging but is often necessary to protect one's emotional well-being.

In the journey toward understanding and healing, it is helpful to approach these situations with compassion—for oneself and, if possible, for the emotionally immature parents. Compassion does not mean accepting hurtful behaviors but rather acknowledging the complex emotional landscape that every individual navigates, often with imperfect tools.

As we move forward, it is essential to consider how the avoidance and denial of emotionally immature parents can escalate into patterns of conflict and criticism, further complicating the family dynamic. By addressing these issues with empathy and insight, we can dismantle the communication barriers and foster a more nurturing and emotionally mature environment.

Conflict and Criticism

In navigating relationships with emotionally immature parents, we often find ourselves entrenched in patterns of conflict and criticism that can feel both bewildering and disheartening. This dynamic is a source of pain and a significant barrier to healthy communication.

When emotionally immature parents face conflict, their responses can be unpredictable and frequently disproportionate to the situation.

Instead of approaching disagreements with a willingness to understand and resolve, these parents may react defensively, perceiving any form of dissent as a personal attack. This defensiveness can manifest as a barrage of criticism, often leaving their children devalued and misunderstood.

Criticism from a parent, especially when it is constant and harsh, can profoundly impact a child's self-esteem. It can create an environment where the child feels perpetually on trial, always preparing a defense for their actions and choices. This relentless scrutiny can foster a sense of walking on eggshells, where open and honest communication is replaced by a strategy of avoidance or placation to prevent further criticism.

Moreover, emotionally immature parents may lack the self-awareness to recognize the effects of their critical behavior. They might justify their actions as a form of 'tough love' or necessary guidance, not realizing the emotional toll it takes on their children. This lack of insight into their behavior and its repercussions can make it difficult for their children to broach the subject without inciting further conflict.

In these circumstances, children may adopt roles that do not align with their true selves merely to appease their parents and avoid confrontation. This can lead to a suppression of their own needs and desires, which, over time, can result in a loss of personal identity and agency.

The challenge, then, is to navigate this minefield of criticism to preserve one's sense of self while attempting to maintain a relationship with the parent. It requires a delicate balance of asserting one's needs and perspectives without exacerbating the cycle of conflict and criticism.

To move forward, developing strategies for self-protection and self-care becomes essential, including setting boundaries, seeking support from others, and finding constructive ways to express one's needs and desires. It is a journey that involves recognizing the limitations of the parent's emotional capacity while also honoring one's emotional well-being.

In the subsequent exploration of our journey, we will delve into the intricacies of expressing needs and desires in the shadow of emotionally immature parents, seeking pathways to authentic communication and self-expression.

Expressing Needs and Desires

In the realm of family dynamics, mainly when dealing with emotionally immature parents, the ability to effectively express needs and desires often becomes a convoluted endeavor. The communication barriers that arise in such relationships can be both subtle and profound, influencing the immediate interactions and the long-term emotional well-being of the children involved.

When a child attempts to convey their needs to an emotionally immature parent, they may encounter a range of dismissive responses. These parents might respond with indifference, irritation, or even mockery, which sends a clear message to the child that their needs are not of paramount importance. Over time, this invalidation pattern can lead to a deep sense of being misunderstood and neglected.

The challenge here is multifaceted. On the one hand, children of emotionally immature parents often learn to suppress their desires, adapting to the emotional landscape by becoming excessively self-reliant or by mirroring the emotional detachment of their caregivers. On the other hand, these children might also engage in heightened emotional displays, hoping that their increased efforts will finally break through the barriers and elicit the desired response from their parents.

However, such strategies rarely yield the connection and understanding they seek. Emotionally immature parents, by nature, struggle with empathy and are often preoccupied with their own emotional experiences. This self-focus can make it difficult for them to recognize and respond to the emotional cues of others, including their children. Consequently, children may feel that their emotional needs are unmet and entirely unseen.

To navigate this complex terrain, it is essential for children, and later as adults, to develop a keen awareness of their own emotional needs and to cultivate the skills necessary to articulate them. This often requires external support, such as therapy or guidance from emotionally mature mentors, to learn how to express themselves in a manner that is both clear and self-affirming.

Moreover, finding alternative sources of emotional support outside the family unit can be crucial. Establishing relationships with friends, partners, or community members who demonstrate emotional maturity can provide a contrasting experience where the expression of needs and desires is not only accepted but encouraged.

In seeking these healthier dynamics, individuals learn that their emotional needs are valid and that expressing them is not only permissible but necessary for their psychological health. They also understand that while they may not be able to change the emotional immaturity of their parents, they can change how they interact with them and set boundaries to protect their well-being.

Ultimately, the journey of expressing needs and desires in the context of emotionally immature parents is one of self-discovery and empowerment. It is about finding one's voice amid silence and learning to speak one's truth, even when it might not be heard by those we most crave acknowledgment. It is a testament to the resilience of the human spirit and the enduring quest for emotional connection and understanding.

The Struggle for Autonomy

When dealing with emotionally immature parents, children often find themselves in a silent tug-of-war for autonomy. This struggle is not marked by overt confrontations but by subtle yet profound undercurrents of control and resistance. Autonomy – the right to self-governance and independence – becomes a battleground where communication often falters, and barriers are erected, sometimes unwittingly.

For the child of an emotionally immature parent, the quest for autonomy can feel like an uphill battle. The parent may often unconsciously perceive the child's growing independence as a threat to their sense of control or self-worth. They might employ tactics that undermine the child's confidence and decision-making abilities. This can manifest in various ways, such as dismissing the child's opinions, overruling their choices, or using guilt to manipulate them into compliance.

The child's natural desire for parental approval and love further complicates the struggle for autonomy. This desire can create a conflict within the child, torn between asserting their individuality and preserving the emotional bond with their parent. The child may self-censor, suppress their true desires, or second-guess their instincts to maintain peace or avoid the emotional fallout that often accompanies attempts at self-assertion.

Moreover, the child may internalize the belief that their value is contingent upon meeting their parent's expectations or needs. This can lead to a people-pleasing behavior that extends beyond the family unit and into other areas of life, such as friendships and romantic relationships. The child learns to prioritize others' needs over their own, a habit that can be difficult to unlearn and hinder the development of a healthy, autonomous self.

In the context of communication, these dynamics create barriers that are not easily dismantled. The child may struggle to articulate their needs or assert boundaries for fear of reprisal or rejection. Conversations about personal goals or life choices can become fraught with tension, as the emotionally immature parent might struggle to engage in a supportive, non-judgmental dialogue.

It is essential for those grappling with these challenges to recognize that the journey toward autonomy is both necessary and deserving of pursuit. It involves setting boundaries, which is not an act of defiance but a step towards healthy self-respect. It requires patience and self-compassion, as the path is often strewn with setbacks and self-doubt. And it may necessitate seeking support from others who can provide the validation and encouragement that the emotionally immature parent cannot offer.

Ultimately, the struggle for autonomy is a testament to the human spirit's resilience. It is about finding one's voice in the face of silence, claiming one's space where there is overreach, and nurturing one's sense of self in an environment that may not always recognize its worth. It is a profoundly personal yet universally understood aspect of the human experience – the right to define and express oneself freely and authentically.

Chapter Summary

- Emotionally immature parents communicate indirectly, leaving children guessing their intentions and feelings.
- These parents may trivialize their children's emotions, teaching them to doubt and suppress their feelings.
- Blame-shifting is expected, with parents deflecting responsibility to their children instead of accepting accountability.
- Parents use projection to accuse children of having motives or emotions that reflect the parent's issues.
- Communication inconsistency from parents creates an unstable environment, making children feel they must tread carefully.
- Avoidance and denial by parents prevent open dialogue and emotional honesty, leaving children feeling unseen and unheard.
- Conflict and criticism from parents can be disproportionate and defensive, damaging children's self-esteem and sense of self.
- The child's desire for approval complicates the struggle for autonomy, leading to self-censorship and people-pleasing behavior.

5

BOUNDARIES AND EMOTIONAL IMMATURITY

Understanding Boundaries

Boundaries are the invisible lines that define the limits of how we expect to be treated by others. They are essential for healthy relationships and a strong sense of self. When it comes to emotionally immature parents, understanding boundaries becomes exceptionally crucial. These parents may not recognize or respect their children's boundaries due to their emotional needs and insecurities. This lack of boundary recognition can lead to a dynamic where children feel responsible for their parent's emotional well-being, often at their own expense.

Boundaries are frequently blurred or disregarded in a household where emotional immaturity prevails. Children may find that their personal space, feelings, and thoughts are not given the respect they deserve. This can manifest in parents sharing too much of their issues with their children, expecting their children to cater to their emotional states, or dismissing their children's need for privacy and autonomy.

The establishment of boundaries is a developmental milestone. As children grow, they learn to say 'no' and to understand that their feelings and needs are valid and essential. However, children may struggle to develop this critical skill when a parent does not model healthy boundaries. They may feel that their needs are secondary to their parents' and that asserting themselves is an act of defiance or a cause for guilt.

For children of emotionally immature parents, setting boundaries can be fraught with anxiety. There is often a deeply ingrained fear that asserting their needs will lead to rejection or punishment. This fear can persist into adulthood, making it challenging for these individuals to advocate for themselves in other relationships, whether personal or professional.

Children risk becoming entangled with their parents' emotional states without clear boundaries. This enmeshment can lead to a lack of differentiation, where children need help identifying where their parents' feelings end and begin. As a result, they may become hyper-attuned to the needs and moods of others, often at the cost of their emotional health.

It is also important to note that boundaries are not just about saying no; they are also about saying yes to the things that affirm our well-being. They allow us to choose what we let into our lives and what we keep out. When children learn that their boundaries are not respected, they may also struggle to understand healthy relationships and seek out or maintain those relationships.

Without boundaries, children may develop coping mechanisms that can be detrimental in the long run. They might become people-pleasers, constantly seeking approval and validation from others, or swing to the other extreme, becoming overly rigid and distant to protect themselves from further emotional intrusion.

Understanding boundaries is the first step towards healing from the impact of growing up with emotionally immature parents. It is about recognizing the right to one's feelings, thoughts, and needs. It is about learning to assert oneself in a way that is respectful to both self and others. And ultimately, it is about creating a life where one can thrive, not just survive, despite the challenges of the past.

The Consequences of Poor Boundaries

Children raised by emotionally immature parents may find themselves in the precarious position of navigating a world without clear limits or guidelines. The lack of boundaries can manifest in several ways, each with challenges and repercussions.

One of the most immediate consequences is the role reversal often observed in these families. Children may feel compelled to take on adult responsibilities, becoming caretakers for their parents' emotional well-being. This role reversal sometimes referred to as parentification, can burden a child with undue stress and rob them of a carefree childhood. It can also lead to an underdeveloped sense of self, as the child's needs and desires are consistently sidelined in favor of the parents.

Furthermore, children may need clear boundaries to develop a robust sense of autonomy. They might find it challenging to recognize where they end and others begin, leading to difficulties forming healthy relationships later in life. This enmeshment can result in a lack of personal identity and an over-reliance on others for validation and self-worth.

The emotional volatility often present in homes with emotionally immature parents can also create an environment of unpredictability. Children may become hyper-vigilant, constantly on guard for their parent's next outburst or emotional need. This state of heightened alertness can lead to anxiety and stress, which, if left unchecked, can persist into adulthood.

In addition, the absence of boundaries may leave children vulnerable to manipulation. Emotionally immature parents may use guilt, withdrawal of affection, or other manipulative tactics to maintain control or avoid dealing with their issues. This manipulation can sow seeds of confusion in children, making it difficult to trust their feelings and perceptions.

The consequences of poor boundaries extend beyond the immediate family as well. Social interactions may be fraught with misunderstandings, as these children might either lack the ability to assert themselves or do so in an overly aggressive or confrontational way. The balance of give-and-take in relationships can be elusive, leading to a pattern of one-sided friendships or romantic partnerships.

It is essential to recognize that the impact of growing up with emotionally immature parents is not a life sentence. Awareness is the first step toward change. By understanding the consequences of poor boundaries, individuals can begin the process of healing and growth. They can learn to establish and maintain healthy boundaries, which will be explored in the forthcoming discussion, and in doing so, they can reclaim their sense of self and build more fulfilling relationships.

Setting and Maintaining Healthy Boundaries

In the journey of personal growth, setting and maintaining healthy boundaries emerges as a pivotal skill. Boundaries are the invisible lines we draw around ourselves to protect our well-being and define what is acceptable and not in our relationships. They are essential in fostering respect, understanding, and a sense of individuality.

When dealing with emotionally immature parents, establishing boundaries can be particularly challenging. These parents may have never learned to respect the personal space and autonomy of others, often because their boundaries were not respected during their formative years. As a result, they might intrude upon, dismiss, or even ridicule the boundaries their children attempt to set. This can lead to a cycle of frustration and resentment, which, if left unaddressed, can severely strain the parent-child relationship.

To set boundaries with emotionally immature parents, it is crucial first to identify what you value and need in your relationship with them. Reflect on the areas where you feel discomfort, anger, or sadness. These emotions are often indicators that a boundary has been crossed. It might be the expectation that you will always put their needs before your own or the lack of privacy in your personal life. Once you pinpoint these areas, you can begin articulating your boundaries.

Communicating your boundaries clearly and assertively is the next step. This does not mean being aggressive or confrontational. Instead, it involves expressing your needs calmly and firmly. For example, "I value our time together, but I need some time for myself. Let's schedule our calls once a week instead of every day." It's essential to use "I" statements, which focus on your feelings and needs, rather than "you" statements, which can be accusatory.

Expect resistance. Emotionally immature parents may not readily accept your boundaries. They might react with confusion, anger, or guilt-tripping tactics. It's essential to remain consistent and not to give in to emotional manipulation. This is where maintaining the boundaries you've set becomes vital. Consistency conveys that you are serious about your needs and expect them to be respected.

It can be helpful to establish consequences for boundary violations. These should not be punitive but rather actions you will take to protect your well-being. For instance, if a parent continues to call you multiple times a day after you've asked for space, you might decide not to answer the phone outside of the agreed-upon times.

Self-care is an integral part of maintaining boundaries. It can be emotionally taxing to navigate these dynamics, and nurturing yourself in the process is essential. This might involve seeking support from friends, a therapist, or support groups where you can share your experiences and learn from others who have faced similar challenges.

Remember, setting and maintaining boundaries is not an act of self-ishness; it is an act of self-respect. It allows you to engage with your parents from a place of strength and stability rather than compliance and resentment. It is a step towards a healthier, more balanced relationship where both parties can interact with mutual respect and understanding.

Dealing with Resistance

As you embark on the journey of setting and maintaining healthy boundaries with emotionally immature parents, it is almost inevitable that you will encounter resistance. This resistance can manifest in various forms, from subtle guilt-tripping to outright anger and denial. It is a natural reaction, as boundaries can challenge long-standing family dynamics and power structures. Understanding and navigating this resistance is crucial for your emotional well-being and the health of your relationship with your parents.

When dealing with resistance, it's essential to recognize that emotionally immature individuals often struggle with self-reflection and may have a limited capacity for empathy. Their responses to boundary-setting are not necessarily personal attacks but reflections of their emotional regulation and understanding of limitations. They might perceive your boundaries as a form of rejection or criticism, which can trigger defensive behaviors.

One common form of resistance is the emotional plea. Your parent may express hurt feelings or sadness to persuade you to retract your boundaries. While listening and validating genuine emotions is essential, it is equally important to remain firm in your decisions. Compassion does not require you to sacrifice your needs; it means acknowledging their feelings while also honoring your own.

Another form of resistance is denial. Your parent may deny that there is a problem or that your boundaries are necessary. They might insist that you are misinterpreting their actions or being too sensitive. In these instances, having clear examples of behaviors that necessitate the boundaries is helpful. Communicate your experiences calmly and assertively without expecting them to understand or agree immediately.

Sometimes, resistance can escalate to anger or blame. Your parent may accuse you of being selfish, ungrateful, or disrespectful. In the face of such accusations, it is crucial to remain calm and not engage in a power struggle. Reiterate your boundaries, focusing on your needs and feelings, using "I" statements to avoid sounding accusatory.

It's also possible that your parent will test your boundaries, consciously or unconsciously, to see if they are firm. Consistency is critical in these moments. Each time a boundary is tested, calmly reaffirm it. This conveys that your boundaries are not negotiable, and you are committed to upholding them.

Sometimes, you may need to implement consequences if your boundaries are repeatedly disregarded. This could mean reducing contact or taking a break from the relationship until your parent is willing to respect your boundaries. While this can be a painful step to take, it is sometimes necessary for your mental health and the possibility of a healthier relationship in the future.

Remember, setting boundaries is not an act of aggression; it is an act of self-respect and self-care. It is about creating a relationship dynamic for mutual respect and emotional safety. As you navigate the resistance from your emotionally immature parents, it is essential to seek support from friends, therapists, or support groups. They can give you the encouragement and perspective needed to stay the course.

Dealing with resistance is a testament to your strength and commitment to well-being. It is a complex but essential step in fostering a healthier dynamic with your parents, where your emotional needs are acknowledged and respected.

Chapter Summary

- Boundaries define how we expect to be treated; they're crucial for healthy relationships and self-identity, especially with emotionally immature parents who may not respect their children's boundaries.
- Children in homes with emotionally immature parents often experience blurred boundaries, leading to a lack of respect for their personal space, feelings, and autonomy.
- The development of boundaries is a milestone; children with emotionally immature parents may struggle to assert their needs, feeling responsible for their parent's emotions.

- Setting boundaries can cause anxiety for these children, fearing rejection or punishment, and this fear can extend into their adult relationships.
- Without clear boundaries, children risk becoming entangled with their parents' emotions, leading to difficulty differentiating their feelings from their parents'.
- Boundaries are about saying yes to what affirms our well-being; children with poor boundaries may struggle to recognize and maintain healthy relationships.
- Poor boundaries can lead to detrimental coping mechanisms, such as people-pleasing or becoming overly rigid to protect oneself from emotional harm.
- Understanding and asserting boundaries is the first step towards healing from the impact of emotionally immature parents, allowing individuals to thrive despite past challenges.

6

THE EMOTIONAL TOOLBOX

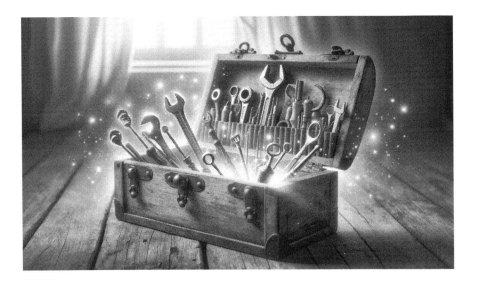

Self-Awareness and Emotional Intelligence

Growing up with emotionally immature parents can often leave children without a clear roadmap for navigating their emotional landscapes. As adults, these children may find themselves at a loss when understanding and managing their feelings. This is where self-awareness and emotional intelligence become a cornerstone for personal growth and healing.

Self-awareness is the ability to recognize and understand your moods, emotions, and drives and their effect on others. On the other hand, emotional intelligence is the capacity to be aware of, control, and express one's emotions and handle interpersonal relationships judiciously and empathetically. Both are essential tools for anyone, but they are particularly vital for those who have experienced the challenges of emotionally immature parenting.

To begin cultivating self-awareness, creating a space for introspection is essential. This can be achieved through journaling, meditation, or therapy. These activities encourage a dialogue with oneself, allowing for a deeper understanding of personal emotional triggers and patterns. Recognizing these patterns is the first step toward change. For instance, you might feel particularly anxious when faced with uncertainty. This trait could stem from the unpredictability of an emotionally immature parent's reactions.

Emotional intelligence involves more than just recognizing your own emotions; it also includes understanding the emotions of others. For those raised by emotionally immature parents, this can be a complex task. These parents may not have modeled empathy or dismissed or invalidated their children's feelings, making it difficult for them to learn how to empathize effectively. However, with conscious effort, one can learn to listen actively and respond to others with sensitivity and understanding.

One practical method to enhance emotional intelligence is practicing active conversation listening. This means fully concentrating on what is being said rather than passively hearing the speaker's message. It involves listening with all senses and giving full attention to the speaker. This practice can help in recognizing the emotions behind words and responding to them appropriately.

Another critical aspect of emotional intelligence is the ability to regulate one's own emotions. This means not only understanding how you feel but also how to respond to those feelings in a way that is constructive rather than destructive. Deep breathing, mindfulness, and cognitive restructuring can help manage emotional responses. For example, when feeling overwhelmed, taking a moment to breathe deeply and center oneself can prevent a reactive and potentially harmful response.

It is also beneficial to cultivate a vocabulary for emotions. Many people raised by emotionally immature parents were not taught how to express their feelings and may struggle to identify what they are feeling beyond basic emotions like happiness, sadness, or anger. Expanding one's emotional vocabulary can provide a more nuanced understanding of one's emotional state, leading to more effective communication and self-regulation.

Developing self-awareness and emotional intelligence is a journey that requires patience, practice, and self-compassion. It is about building skills that can lead to a more fulfilling and emotionally rich life. As you learn to navigate your emotional world with greater ease, you will be better equipped to manage the complexities of relationships, including those with emotionally immature parents.

Managing Emotions

In understanding emotionally immature parents, we have explored the importance of self-awareness and emotional intelligence. Now, let's delve into the practical strategies for managing emotions, which is a critical component of the emotional toolbox we are equipping ourselves with.

Emotionally immature parents often struggle with managing their own emotions, which can lead to a tumultuous family environment. As their child, whether you are an adolescent or an adult, you may find yourself frequently on the receiving end of emotional outbursts or cold indifference. It is essential, then, to learn how to navigate these waters with grace and resilience.

Firstly, it is essential to recognize that you cannot control your parents' emotions. Still, you can control your responses to them. Begin by identifying your emotional triggers and your typical responses to your parents' behaviors. Awareness is the first step towards change, and by understanding your patterns, you can break free from reactive cycles.

Once you grasp your triggers, you can employ techniques to manage your emotional responses. Deep breathing, mindfulness, and meditation are powerful tools that can help calm your nervous system and provide a buffer against immediate reactions. When faced with an emotionally charged situation, take a moment to breathe deeply and center yourself. This pause allows you to choose a more thoughtful and composed response.

Another critical strategy is setting healthy boundaries. Boundaries are not about changing the other person but about respecting your needs and limits. Communicate your boundaries to your parents in a firm yet compassionate manner. It is okay to say no, to ask for space, or to decline participation in conversations that you find emotionally draining.

It is also beneficial to seek out support systems outside of your family. Friends, mentors, support groups, or therapists can provide a sounding board and offer guidance. They can help you process your emotions, reinforce your boundaries, and remind you of your worth when your parents' immaturity makes you question it.

Lastly, practice self-compassion. Growing up with emotionally immature parents can leave you with a harsh inner critic. It is crucial to be kind to yourself, acknowledge your feelings, and recognize that you are doing your best in a challenging situation. Self-compassion is not self-pity; it is about treating yourself with the same kindness and understanding that you would offer a good friend.

By incorporating these strategies into your emotional toolbox, you can cultivate a sense of emotional autonomy and resilience. While you cannot change your parents' past or behavior, you can empower yourself to navigate your emotional world with more excellent skill and confidence. As we build upon these tools, we will explore how empathy can further enhance our relationships and our understanding of emotionally immature parents.

The Power of Empathy

Empathy is vital in the emotional toolbox, especially when dealing with emotionally immature parents. It is the bridge that connects us to another person's inner world, allowing us to understand their feelings and perspectives. When we cultivate empathy, we deepen our emotional intelligence and create a space for healing and understanding in our relationships.

For those who have grown up with emotionally immature parents, empathy might not have been modeled effectively. These parents may have struggled to attune to their children's emotional needs, often because their emotional development was stunted early due to their experiences or inherent personality traits. As a result, their children might have felt misunderstood, invalidated, or emotionally neglected.

However, as adults, we can develop empathy that we may not have received. This begins with self-empathy—recognizing and validating our own emotions. By acknowledging our feelings and treating ourselves with kindness and understanding, we set the groundwork for extending empathy to others, including our parents.

Practicing empathy towards emotionally immature parents does not mean excusing their behaviors or neglecting our boundaries. It means looking beyond their actions to the underlying fears, insecurities, and unmet needs that drive their immaturity. This perspective can help us respond to them with compassion rather than react with frustration or anger.

Empathy also empowers us to communicate more effectively. When we approach conversations with an empathetic mindset, we're more likely to express our thoughts and feelings in a way that can be heard and understood. It can also encourage our parents to open up and share more about their experiences, potentially leading to a more authentic connection.

Moreover, empathy has the power to break the cycle of emotional immaturity. By modeling empathetic behavior, we improve our emotional health and influence those around us. Children who observe empathetic interactions are more likely to develop solid emotional skills, ensuring that the next generation is better equipped to handle the complexities of emotional life.

In embracing empathy, we must also recognize its limits. Sometimes, our empathy may not be reciprocated or appreciated despite our best efforts. In such instances, it's essential to maintain our emotional boundaries and practice self-care. Empathy should not come at the cost of our well-being.

Empathy stands out as a transformative tool as we continue to build our emotional toolbox. It allows us to connect with others more profoundly and fosters a more compassionate world. By integrating empathy into our daily lives, we improve our relationships with emotionally immature parents and enhance our overall emotional resilience and adaptability.

Resilience and Adaptability

Growing up with emotionally immature parents can feel like navigating a ship in unpredictable waters. The unpredictable moods, the lack of emotional support, and the role reversal where the child becomes the caretaker can lead to a tumultuous inner world. However, amidst these challenges lies the opportunity for developing a profound level of resilience and adaptability—two indispensable tools in the emotional toolbox that can be honed to navigate life's complexities.

Resilience is the ability to bounce back from difficulties, recover strength, and progress despite emotional setbacks. For children of emotionally immature parents, resilience becomes a survival skill. The inner force allows them to emerge from the chaos of their upbringing not just intact but often with a unique strength. This strength is characterized by a deep understanding that they can endure much and still find ways to thrive.

Adaptability, on the other hand, is the capacity to adjust to new conditions. When the emotional landscape of home is ever-shifting, adaptability becomes second nature. Children learn to read the room, anticipate the unpredictable, and mold themselves in ways that can minimize conflict or emotional distress. While this skill is developed under less-than-ideal circumstances, it can be a powerful asset later in life, allowing individuals to navigate change with grace and flexibility.

To cultivate resilience, one must first acknowledge the reality of their situation. It involves a conscious decision not to be defined by the limitations of one's parents. This means recognizing that while you cannot change the past, you can influence your reaction to it and your path forward. It is about finding and focusing on the aspects of life you can control, such as your beliefs, choices, and actions.

Building resilience also involves fostering a sense of self-worth independent of parental validation. It means setting personal boundaries and learning to say no, which can be particularly challenging for those who have been conditioned to put their parents' emotional needs first. It's about understanding that self-care is not selfish but essential to maintaining one's emotional health.

Adaptability is enhanced through accepting change as an inherent part of life. It requires a willingness to let go of rigid expectations and embrace the idea that there is more than one way to achieve a goal or to find happiness. For the adult child of emotionally immature parents, it means learning to trust their instincts and make decisions based on their values rather than constantly seeking approval or direction from others.

Resilience and adaptability are nurtured through supportive relationships with friends, mentors, or a therapeutic community. These connections can provide the encouragement and feedback necessary to reinforce an individual's sense of self and to help them navigate the complexities of their emotions and relationships.

In essence, resilience and adaptability are about surviving the storm and learning to dance in the rain. They are about recognizing that while we cannot control the weather, we can adjust our sails. For those who have grown up with emotionally immature parents, these skills are not just theoretical concepts but lived experiences that shape their approach to life's challenges and opportunities.

As we explore the emotional toolbox, it becomes clear that the tools we gather are interconnected. The resilience and adaptability we develop in response to our upbringing can be further enhanced by cultivating mindfulness and presence, allowing us to live more fully in the moment and engage with our lives and relationships more meaningfully.

Mindfulness and Presence

In navigating the complex emotional landscape that comes with having emotionally immature parents, it's essential to develop an array of coping strategies. One such strategy, which can be particularly transformative, is the practice of mindfulness and presence.

Mindfulness is fully engaging with the present moment without judgment or distraction. It is about experiencing life with an open heart and a clear mind as it unfolds. For those who have grown up with emotionally immature parents, mindfulness can be a beacon of stability in the often tumultuous waves of emotional unpredictability.

When practicing mindfulness, we learn to observe our thoughts and feelings without getting entangled. This is crucial when dealing with emotionally immature parents, who may often project their feelings onto us or create an environment where emotional reactions are heightened and unpredictable. By cultivating mindfulness, we can create a space between stimulus and response, allowing us to choose how we react to our parents' behaviors.

Presence, a companion to mindfulness, is about being fully attuned to the here and now. It means engaging with our environment and its people with our full attention. For adults who have emotionally immature parents, presence can be a powerful tool. It allows us to interact with our parents without being hijacked by past grievances or future anxieties. It helps us to maintain our emotional boundaries and engage in conversations without being pulled into old patterns of conflict or emotional neglect.

The practice of mindfulness and presence begins with simple steps. It can be as straightforward as taking a few deep breaths before responding to a parent's comment that might otherwise trigger an automatic reaction. It might involve a daily meditation, where we sit quietly and observe our thoughts, learning to let them pass without attachment. Or it could be a mindful walk, where we focus intently on the sensations of our body moving and the environment around us.

As we become more adept at these practices, we notice a shift in our interactions with our parents. We may be less reactive and more compassionate with them and ourselves. We might discover a newfound patience and a greater capacity for listening and understanding, even when faced with emotional immaturity.

Moreover, mindfulness and presence can help us to appreciate the good moments, no matter how small, and to find joy and gratitude in our relationships. They teach us to live with peace and acceptance, knowing that while we cannot change our parents, we can change our relationship experience.

In essence, mindfulness and presence are not just practices but a way of life—a way to navigate the complex emotional waters with grace, strength, and stability. They are essential tools in our emotional toolbox, helping us build a responsive rather than reactive life grounded in a deep sense of self-awareness and self-care.

Chapter Summary

- Growing up with emotionally immature parents can hinder a child's ability to manage emotions, necessitating the development of self-awareness and emotional intelligence.
- Self-awareness involves recognizing one's emotions and their impact on others. In contrast, emotional intelligence includes understanding and regulating emotions and empathizing with others.
- Cultivating self-awareness can be achieved through introspection practices like journaling, meditation, or therapy, which help identify emotional triggers and patterns.
- Emotional intelligence can be enhanced by practicing active listening and learning to regulate emotional responses using deep breathing and mindfulness techniques.
- Expanding one's emotional vocabulary is essential for those who weren't taught to express their feelings, leading to more effective communication and self-regulation.
- Managing emotions involves recognizing that one cannot control one's parents' emotions but can control one's

responses, employing techniques like deep breathing and setting healthy boundaries.

- Empathy is crucial for understanding emotionally immature parents, allowing for compassion and improved communication. Still, it should not come at the cost of one's well-being.
- Resilience and adaptability, developed through challenging upbringings, involve recognizing one's ability to bounce back and adjust to new conditions, supported by healthy relationships and self-care.

7

HEALING FROM EMOTIONAL IMMATURITY

The Journey to Healing

Growing up with emotionally immature parents can leave deep-seated marks that often go unrecognized for years. As adults, the journey to healing from these childhood experiences is necessary and challenging.

It requires a compassionate understanding of oneself and the courage to confront and reconcile with the past.

The first step on this path is the acknowledgment of the pain and confusion that emotionally immature parenting can cause. It's essential to recognize that the feelings of neglect, misunderstanding, or emotional abandonment are valid and significant. This recognition is not about assigning blame but about understanding the context of your emotional world.

Once acknowledgment has taken place, the next phase involves self-compassion. It's about offering yourself the kindness and patience you may not have received as a child. Self-compassion is a nurturing practice that allows you to create a safe emotional space for healing. It involves treating yourself with the same care and understanding that you would offer a good friend.

Another vital aspect of healing is setting boundaries. Boundaries are the guidelines you set for yourself and others regarding acceptable behavior. They are crucial in protecting your emotional well-being. For those who have grown up with emotionally immature parents, learning to establish and maintain healthy boundaries can be a transformative experience. It empowers you to control your interactions and advocate for your needs.

Developing emotional literacy is also a vital component of the healing journey. Emotional literacy is identifying, expressing, and managing emotions effectively. It's about becoming fluent in the language of emotions, which may have been discouraged or ignored in your upbringing. By enhancing your emotional literacy, you can better navigate your feelings and the feelings of others, leading to more fulfilling and authentic relationships.

Furthermore, seeking support through therapy or support groups can be an invaluable part of the healing process. A therapist can provide a safe, non-judgmental space to explore your experiences and emotions. They can offer guidance and strategies to help you cope with the lingering effects of emotional immaturity from your parents. Support groups can also offer a sense of community and understanding from others who have had similar experiences.

Lastly, it's essential to cultivate a life that reflects your values, desires, and needs. This might involve pursuing passions previously set aside or creating a chosen family of friends and loved ones who provide the emotional connection and support you deserve. By building a life that honors your true self, you can find fulfillment and joy that extends beyond the shadow of the past.

The journey to healing from the impact of emotionally immature parents is not a linear one. It is filled with complexities and nuances unique to each individual's experiences. However, with each step taken towards understanding, compassion, and self-care, the path becomes more apparent, leading to a more grounded and emotionally resilient self.

Therapeutic Approaches

As we navigate the complexities of healing from the wounds inflicted by emotionally immature parents, it is essential to explore the various therapeutic approaches that can facilitate this profoundly personal journey. These approaches are not one-size-fits-all; they offer a spectrum of strategies tailored to the individual's experiences and needs.

One of the most effective therapeutic approaches is individual psychotherapy. In this confidential space, a trained therapist can help you understand the roots of your emotional pain and the impact of your parents' immaturity on your development. Through techniques such as cognitive-behavioral therapy (CBT), you can learn to challenge and reframe the negative beliefs about yourself that may have been instilled during childhood. CBT can also provide you with tools to cope with anxiety, depression, and other emotional difficulties that often accompany the experience of being raised by emotionally immature parents.

Another approach that has proven beneficial is group therapy. Sharing your story with others with similar experiences can be incredibly validating and empowering. It helps to know you are not alone in your struggles. Group therapy provides a supportive environment where you can learn from the experiences of others, gain different perspectives, and practice new ways of relating to people in a safe setting.

For some, family therapy might be an option, mainly if there is a willingness from the family to acknowledge past issues and work together toward healing. This form of therapy can facilitate open communication, help resolve conflicts, and teach family members healthier ways of interacting with one another. However, it is essential to note that family therapy is not suitable for everyone, especially if there is ongoing abuse or a complete lack of willingness to change from emotionally immature parents.

Mindfulness and meditation practices can also be incorporated into the healing process. These practices help develop a greater awareness of the present moment. They can be instrumental in managing stress and emotional regulation. By observing your thoughts and feelings without judgment, you can break the cycle of reactivity that may have been a survival mechanism in your childhood environment.

Art therapy is another avenue through which many find healing. It offers a non-verbal outlet for expressing complex emotions. It can benefit those who struggle to articulate their feelings through words. Through the creative process, you may discover insights about yourself and your past that were previously obscured.

Lastly, self-help and educational resources can complement therapeutic approaches. Books, workshops, and online content focused on overcoming the challenges of emotionally immature parents can provide additional support and guidance. These resources can help you understand that your experiences are part of a larger narrative shared by many and that recovery is possible and within reach.

Each of these therapeutic approaches can be a stepping stone toward healing. It is important to remember that the process is not linear and may require trying different methods to find what resonates with you. The ultimate goal is to build a life defined not by the limitations of the past but by the possibilities of a future where emotional maturity and well-being are within your control.

Forgiveness and Letting Go

In the journey toward healing,, there comes a pivotal moment when one must confront the concept of forgiveness and the act of letting go. This is not a straightforward path, nor is it one that can be rushed or prescribed in a uniform way for everyone. However, it is crucial to reclaim one's emotional well-being and autonomy.

In this context, forgiveness is not about condoning the hurtful behavior of parents who may have been emotionally unavailable or erratic. It is not about absolving them of responsibility or pretending that the pain they caused did not matter. Instead, forgiveness is an internal process, releasing the burden of carrying anger, resentment, or a desire for retribution. It is a personal liberation from the emotional shackles that bind one to the past.

Forgiveness is acknowledging the whole reality of what occurred and accepting that it cannot be changed. It is to understand that emotionally immature parents, in many cases, were limited by their psychological struggles and may not have been capable of providing the emotional support their children needed. This understanding does not excuse their actions but provides a context that can help mitigate the sting of personal insult.

Letting go is the natural companion to forgiveness. It involves the conscious decision to stop allowing past grievances to dictate one's emotional state and life choices. Letting go shifts focus from what has been lost to what can be created anew. It is about moving forward with the lessons learned and the strength gained from surviving and transcending past adversity.

The process of forgiveness and letting go is deeply personal and often nonlinear. It may involve moments of profound insight and periods of backsliding into old patterns of resentment. It is essential to approach this process with patience and self-compassion, understanding that healing is not a destination but a continual journey.

As one works through these emotional complexities, engaging in practices that nurture the self and reinforce the commitment to personal growth is helpful. These may include mindfulness meditation, journaling, or creative expression—anything that allows for reflection and the constructive processing of emotions.

Ultimately, forgiveness and letting go are acts of self-care. They free individuals from the weight of past hurts and empower them to build a life defined not by what has been endured but by what one chooses to cultivate in its aftermath. This is the foundation upon which one can begin to rebuild the self, constructing an identity rooted in the present and looking toward the future with hope and resilience.

Rebuilding the Self

Growing up with emotionally immature parents can leave deep imprints on one's sense of self. The journey of healing is not just about moving past the pain but also about reconstructing a self-identity that may have been neglected or distorted through years of emotional turbulence. This reconstruction is a process of self-discovery, self-compassion, and self-empowerment.

The first step in rebuilding the self is to understand that your worth is not contingent on the approval or understanding of your parents. This is a challenging realization for many, as the desire for parental validation is deeply ingrained. It's important to acknowledge that your value is intrinsic and not dependent on someone else's ability to recognize it.

Self-discovery involves exploring your interests, desires, and values independent of your parents' influence. It's about asking yourself who you are outside of the role you played in your family. This can be both liberating and daunting, as it may involve entering unfamiliar territory. It's okay to start small, with simple questions like what colors you prefer, what hobbies you enjoy, or what causes you feel passionate about. Over time, these small discoveries can build a more comprehensive picture of your authentic self.

Self-compassion is crucial in this journey. You may have internalized critical voices from your parents, which can lead to self-doubt and self-criticism. Learning to speak to yourself with kindness and understanding is vital to healing. This might involve challenging negative self-talk, practicing mindfulness, or engaging in activities that make you feel nurtured and cared for. Remember, healing is not a linear process, and it's okay to have days where you feel less than your best.

Self-empowerment comes from setting boundaries and advocating for your needs. Emotionally immature parents may not have respected your boundaries in the past. Still, as an adult, you have the right to establish what is acceptable for you. This might mean saying no to demands that compromise your well-being, asking for space, or seeking out reciprocal and respectful relationships. Empowerment also means recognizing that you have the agency to shape your life and make choices that align with your true self.

As you engage in this rebuilding process, seeking out support is essential. This can come from friends, a therapist, support groups, or any safe space where you can express your feelings and experiences without judgment. Surrounding yourself with understanding individuals can provide encouragement and perspective as you navigate the complexities of healing.

In rebuilding the self, you are not erasing your past or the influence of your parents. Instead, you are using what you've learned from your experiences to forge a stronger, more resilient sense of self. You are acknowledging the child you once were, with all their needs and feelings, and committing to being the nurturing presence that child deserves. This is not a journey of forgetting but one of transformation and growth, where the scars of the past become the wisdom of the present.

Creating New Family Dynamics

In the journey toward healing from the wounds inflicted by emotionally immature parents, we have traversed the rugged terrain of self-reconstruction. With newfound strength and self-awareness, we now turn our attention to the delicate task of reshaping the family dynamics that have, for so long, been defined by emotional immaturity.

Creating new family dynamics is not about changing others—futile and outside our control—but changing how we engage with our family. It is about establishing boundaries, communicating effectively, and nurturing our emotional health in the context of these relationships.

The first step in this transformative process is recognizing and accepting that our parents may never fully understand or validate our feelings. This can be a painful realization, but it is also a liberating one. It allows us to stop seeking approval and build a sense of independence from our parents' perceptions.

Next, we must learn the art of boundary-setting. Boundaries are not walls meant to shut others out; they are gates that allow us to interact with others on our terms. They help us to define what is acceptable and what is not, what we are willing to tolerate, and what we are not. When we establish clear boundaries, we communicate to our parents and ourselves that our feelings and needs are valid and essential.

Effective communication is the cornerstone of any relationship, and this holds especially true in the context of emotionally charged family dynamics. We must strive to express our thoughts and feelings calmly and clearly without expecting our parents to always respond in the way we hope. It is also crucial to listen actively, trying to understand our parents' perspective, even if we disagree. This does not mean we condone their emotional immaturity, but rather that we acknowledge it as a part of the reality we must navigate.

Creating new family dynamics may mean limiting contact or taking time away from family interactions. This is not an act of malice but one of self-preservation. It is about giving ourselves the space to grow and heal without being constantly pulled back into the chaos of emotional immaturity.

Finally, it is essential to cultivate a support system outside of our family. Friends, mentors, therapists, and support groups can provide the understanding and encouragement we may not receive from our parents. They can offer perspectives and advice that help us to see our family situation more clearly and to navigate it more effectively.

In creating new family dynamics, we are not discarding our past but redefining our present and future. We are not abandoning our family but are engaging with them in a healthier, more self-respecting manner. This is not a journey we undertake lightly, but it promises a more authentic and fulfilling life. As we continue to heal and grow, we can find peace in the knowledge that we have the power to shape our own lives, regardless of where we started.

Chapter Summary

- Acknowledge the pain caused by emotionally immature parents and understand that feelings of neglect and emotional abandonment are valid.
- Practice self-compassion by offering yourself kindness and patience, creating a safe emotional space for healing.
- Set boundaries to protect emotional well-being and take control of interactions, advocating for personal needs.
- Develop emotional literacy to identify, express, and manage emotions, leading to more authentic relationships.
- Seek support through therapy or support groups to explore emotions and cope with the effects of emotional immaturity.
- Cultivate a life that reflects personal values, desires, and needs, pursuing passions and creating a supportive chosen family.
- Explore various therapeutic approaches tailored to individual needs, such as individual psychotherapy, group therapy, and mindfulness.
- Engage in forgiveness and letting go as acts of self-care, releasing the burden of anger and resentment to move forward.

8

NAVIGATING RELATIONSHIPS WITH EMOTIONALLY IMMATURE PARENTS

Reevaluating the Parent-Child Relationship

In the journey of personal growth, there comes a pivotal moment where reevaluating the parent-child relationship becomes beneficial and necessary. This reevaluation is a process of understanding that the dynamics established in childhood may no longer serve your well-being as an adult. It is a step towards emotional autonomy and healthier interactions.

As you embark on this reevaluation, it is essential to approach it with a blend of honesty and compassion. Begin by acknowledging the reality of your parents' emotional capabilities. Emotionally immature parents often struggle with self-awareness and empathy, which can manifest in their inability to engage in deep, meaningful conversations or to provide the emotional support they may seek. Recognizing these limitations is not an act of condemnation but rather an acceptance of who they are. This acceptance allows you to set realistic expectations for your relationship with them.

In this process, reflecting on how your parents' emotional immaturity has shaped your emotional responses and behaviors is crucial. Have you found yourself adopting specific roles to cope with their immaturity? Perhaps you've become the caretaker, the peacekeeper, or the one who always compromises to avoid conflict. Identifying these patterns can enlighten and empower you to make conscious choices about how you interact with your parents moving forward.

Another aspect of reevaluation is considering the boundaries you need to establish for your mental and emotional well-being. Boundaries are not about pushing your parents away but protecting your inner peace. They can range from deciding how often you communicate with your parents to what topics you choose to discuss with them. Setting boundaries is an act of self-care and is essential in any relationship, especially those with emotionally immature individuals.

As you redefine your relationship with your parents, seeking out and fostering other supportive relationships is equally important. Surrounding yourself with friends, mentors, or counselors who understand and respect your emotional needs can provide a contrast to the dynamics you experience with your parents. These relationships can offer the empathy and maturity that you may not receive from your parents, and they can be a source of strength and validation.

Lastly, it is essential to practice self-compassion throughout this reevaluation. You may experience various emotions, from sadness and anger to relief and hope. These feelings are all valid. Reevaluating your relationship with your parents is not a straightforward path, and it may involve periods of trial and error. Be patient with yourself as you navigate this complex terrain.

By reevaluating your relationship with your parents, you are taking a courageous step toward creating a life that honors your emotional needs and well-being. Remember, this reevaluation is not about finding fault or assigning blame but about understanding the dynamics at play and making informed decisions on how to interact with your parents in a way that is healthiest for you.

Communication Strategies

Communication is a pivotal element in the journey of understanding and interacting with emotionally immature parents. It is a delicate dance that requires patience, clarity, and, often, a redefinition of expectations. The strategies discussed here aim to foster a constructive dialogue, given the unique challenges that emotionally immature parents may present.

Firstly, it is essential to approach conversations with a sense of calm and self-assuredness. Emotionally immature parents may not respond well to confrontation or heightened emotions. Therefore, grounding yourself before engaging in discussions can help maintain a serenity conducive to productive communication.

One effective strategy is to employ "I" statements. This technique involves speaking from your perspective without casting blame. For instance, instead of saying, "You never listen to me," you might say, "I feel unheard when I share my thoughts with you." This approach can minimize defensiveness and open the door to more empathetic exchanges.

Active listening is another critical component. This means genuinely hearing your parents' words without immediately formulating a response or judgment. Reflecting on what you've heard them say can validate their feelings and show that you are engaged in the conversation. For example, "It sounds like you're saying you felt overwhelmed when that happened" can demonstrate understanding and care.

Setting boundaries is often necessary when dealing with emotionally immature parents. It's essential to communicate your limits clearly and consistently. Suppose a conversation becomes too heated or unproductive. In that case, it's okay to say, "I need to step back from this discussion right now, but I'm open to revisiting it later when we're both feeling calmer."

Sometimes, shifting the focus from emotional depth to more practical matters may be beneficial. Emotionally immature parents may struggle with deep emotional conversations, so discussing day-to-day topics or problem-solving can be a way to maintain connection without delving into areas that might trigger conflict or discomfort.

It is also crucial to manage your expectations. You may need to accept that your parents might not be capable of the level of emotional maturity or understanding you desire. This acceptance doesn't mean you lower your standards for how you deserve to be treated, but rather that you recognize the limitations of the relationship and adjust your approach accordingly.

Lastly, consider seeking support for yourself. Whether through therapy, support groups, or trusted friends, having a space to process your feelings and experiences can be invaluable. It can also provide additional strategies and perspectives on navigating the complex terrain of your relationship with your parents.

Communicating with emotionally immature parents requires compassion, self-awareness, and resilience. By employing these strategies, you can create a space for dialogue that respects both your needs and the limitations of your parents' emotional capacities. Remember, the goal is not to change who they are but to find a respectful way to interact and maintain your well-being.

When to Maintain Contact

In the previous section, we explored the delicate art of communication. Let's turn our attention to the considerations that might lead us to maintain contact with our parents despite the challenges their emotional immaturity can present.

Maintaining contact with emotionally immature parents is a deeply personal decision, often rooted in a complex interplay of familial duty, affection, and hope for change. It's essential to recognize that the choice to stay connected does not signify weakness or a lack of awareness. Instead, it can affirm one's values and the desire to uphold family bonds, even when frayed.

One of the primary reasons to maintain contact is the presence of unconditional love. Love, in its purest form, can sometimes transcend the difficulties of emotional immaturity. Your love for your parents motivates you to stay in touch, and this contact does not significantly harm your well-being. This can be a valid reason to sustain the relationship.

Another consideration is the potential for growth and healing. While emotionally immature parents may struggle with change, it is not entirely impossible. With the right communication strategies and boundaries in place, there may be opportunities for small shifts in the relationship dynamics that can lead to more positive interactions over time.

For some, the decision to maintain contact is influenced by practical reasons. This can include financial interdependence, co-parenting grandchildren, or managing family businesses. In such scenarios, contact is not just a personal choice but a practical necessity. Navigating these waters requires a clear set of boundaries and understanding one's limits to prevent emotional drain.

The concept of filial responsibility, deeply ingrained in many cultures, often plays a significant role in the decision to stay connected. The sense of duty to care for one's parents as they age can be a powerful motivator. Suppose this sense of obligation is part of your value system. In that case, finding a balance that honors your beliefs and protects your emotional health is essential.

Lastly, maintaining contact may come from a place of compassion. Recognizing that emotionally immature parents are often dealing with their unresolved issues can lead to a sense of empathy. While this doesn't excuse their behavior, it can provide a context that makes continued contact more manageable.

In all these considerations, assessing this relationship's impact on your life is crucial. It's about finding the proper distance that allows you to engage in a healthy way. This may mean setting firm boundaries, limiting the frequency of contact, or choosing the settings in which you interact with your parents.

Remember, maintaining contact is not about enduring pain for the sake of connection. It's about making an informed choice that aligns with your needs, values, and circumstances. It's a dynamic process that may evolve, requiring you to be reflective and adaptable.

As we move forward, we'll consider the other side of this coin: when it might be necessary to create distance from emotionally immature parents. This is a challenging path to walk, but sometimes, it's necessary for personal well-being and growth.

When to Consider Distance

One of the most challenging decisions you may face is determining whether to create distance in your relationship with emotionally immature parents. This choice is deeply personal and can be fraught with guilt, confusion, and a sense of obligation. However, there are circumstances where establishing boundaries by incorporating distance can be a necessary step for your emotional well-being.

Distance does not necessarily mean cutting off all contact. It can manifest as taking a step back to evaluate the relationship dynamics, reducing the frequency of interactions, or setting firm boundaries around topics of conversation and forms of behavior you find detrimental. The decision to consider distance should be based on a clear understanding of your needs and the patterns of interaction that have historically taken place between you and your parents.

One of the primary reasons to consider distance is the presence of ongoing emotional pain or trauma that is exacerbated by interactions with your parents. Suppose you find yourself repeatedly hurt, disappointed, or emotionally drained after spending time with them. In that case, it may indicate that the relationship impedes your ability to heal and grow.

Another sign that distance may be beneficial is a consistent lack of respect for your boundaries. Emotionally immature parents may struggle with recognizing and honoring their adult children's personal space, beliefs, and choices. Suppose conversations and visits routinely leave you feeling disrespected or violated in your autonomy. In that case, it is worth considering whether the relationship in its current form is healthy for you.

Additionally, notice a pattern of manipulation or emotional blackmail, such as guilt-tripping or passive-aggressive behavior. It may be time to reassess the relationship. These tactics can be particularly damaging, as they often exploit the child's desire for parental approval and love.

It's also important to acknowledge the impact of your parents' emotional immaturity on your other relationships. If maintaining close contact with your parents is causing strain in your romantic partnership, friendships, or parenting, it may be necessary to contemplate distance to protect these other vital connections in your life.

When contemplating distance, it is essential to approach the decision with compassion—not only for yourself but also for your parents. Recognize that their emotional immaturity is likely a result of their unmet needs and unresolved issues. While this understanding does not excuse hurtful behavior, it can help you approach the situation with empathy, reducing the likelihood of unnecessary conflict as you establish boundaries.

It is also crucial to seek support during this time. Whether from friends, a therapist, or a support group, having a network of understanding individuals can give you the strength and perspective to make the best decision for your mental and emotional health.

Ultimately, considering distance is about honoring your needs and nurturing your well-being. It is a step towards breaking the cycle of emotional immaturity and creating a life that is defined not by past pain but by the possibility of a healthier, more fulfilling future.

The Role of Family Therapy

One may reach a point where professional guidance becomes a beacon of hope. Family therapy, a form of psychotherapy that aims to nurture change and development within the family system, can be a valuable resource. It provides a safe space for family members to express their thoughts and feelings. At the same time, a therapist helps navigate the complex emotional landscape.

For those grappling with the challenges posed by emotionally immature parents, family therapy offers a structured environment where each person's perspective is heard and validated. The therapist, trained in managing dynamics where emotional immaturity is present, can facilitate conversations that might otherwise be fraught with misunderstanding and hurt.

In this therapeutic setting, the focus is not on assigning blame but on understanding each family member's emotional world. Emotionally immature parents may struggle with self-awareness and empathy, which can lead to a lack of emotional attunement with their children. A family therapist can help parents explore their childhood experiences, which may have contributed to their emotional development, and how these experiences are reflected in their parenting style.

For adult children, family therapy can be an avenue to articulate their needs and experiences without the fear of retribution or dismissal. It can empower them to establish boundaries and communicate effectively, often for the first time. The therapist can introduce concepts such as emotional intelligence and self-regulation, essential for healthy relationships.

Moreover, family therapy can assist in breaking the cycle of emotional immaturity. By learning new ways of relating and understanding the emotional cues of others, parents can begin to model more mature behaviors. This, in turn, can create a ripple effect, fostering a more emotionally intelligent and resilient family unit.

However, it is essential to note that success in family therapy requires willingness and openness from all parties involved. Emotionally immature parents must be willing to engage in the process and consider the possibility of change. Without this foundational commitment, therapy may become another battleground for family conflict.

In cases where parents are resistant or unable to participate in therapy, individual therapy for the adult child can still be beneficial. It can give them the tools to manage their relationship with their parents and protect their emotional well-being.

Ultimately, family therapy is not a magic cure for the challenges posed by emotionally immature parents. It is a step towards understanding, healing, and possibly transforming strained relationships into ones that are more fulfilling and less fraught with emotional pain. With the guidance of a compassionate therapist, families can embark on a path of growth that honors the complexity of their shared history while forging a healthier emotional future.

Chapter Summary

- Reevaluating the parent-child relationship is crucial for personal growth, especially with emotionally immature parents, to achieve emotional autonomy.
- Acknowledge the limitations of emotionally immature parents, such as a lack of empathy and self-awareness, to set realistic expectations for the relationship.
- Reflect on how your parents' emotional immaturity has influenced your behaviors, like adopting roles of caretaker or peacekeeper, to empower future interactions.
- Establish boundaries for mental and emotional well-being, which is an act of self-care and necessary in relationships with emotionally immature individuals.
- Seek supportive relationships with friends, mentors, or counselors to provide the empathy and maturity lacking in parental relationships.
- Practice self-compassion throughout the reevaluation process, as it involves a range of emotions and is not a straightforward path.
- Communication with emotionally immature parents requires calmness, self-assuredness, strategies like "I" statements, and active listening to foster constructive dialogue.

- Maintaining contact with emotionally immature parents is a personal decision influenced by love, hope for change, practical reasons, cultural duty, and compassion. Still, it requires regular assessment and boundaries to ensure personal well-being.

9

PARENTING AFTER EMOTIONAL IMMATURITY

Breaking the Cycle

The parenting journey is often a mirror, reflecting not just the joys and successes but also the challenges and unresolved issues of our upbringing. For those who have experienced the perplexity and pain of being raised by emotionally immature parents, the path forward can be fraught with uncertainty. How does one ensure that the cycle of emotional immaturity is not perpetuated into the next generation? The answer lies in consciously cultivating emotional intelligence within oneself, thereby rewriting the familial narrative.

Emotional intelligence, at its core, is the ability to recognize, understand, and manage our own emotions and recognize, understand, and influence the emotions of others. It is the cornerstone of healthy, responsive parenting. To break the cycle of emotional immaturity, it is essential to develop the skills that perhaps our parents lacked: empathy, emotional regulation, and the ability to foster secure attachments.

The first step in this transformative process is self-reflection. Take the time to delve into your emotional landscape. Acknowledge the feelings that arise from your childhood experiences, and understand how they have shaped your behavior and reactions. This is not an exercise in blame but rather an opportunity for growth. By identifying the patterns you wish to change, you set the stage for intentional parenting.

Next, commit to learning about and practicing emotional regulation. This means finding healthy ways to cope with stress, frustration, and anger. It involves recognizing when you are becoming emotionally overwhelmed and having strategies to calm yourself. This could be through mindfulness, deep breathing exercises, or even seeking the support of a therapist. As you model emotional regulation, you teach your children to do the same, equipping them with valuable tools for their emotional well-being.

Empathy is another vital component. Strive to see the world through your child's eyes. Validate their feelings, even if they seem trivial to you. Remember, their emotions are as accurate and significant to them as yours are to you. By acknowledging and respecting your child's feelings, you foster an environment of trust and understanding. This empathetic approach allows children to feel heard and supported, which is instrumental in their emotional development.

Lastly, creating secure attachments with your children is paramount. This means being consistently present, both physically and emotionally. It's about offering comfort and security so they know they can rely on you. It's about being responsive to their needs and showing unconditional love. A secure attachment forms the foundation of a child's confidence and self-esteem, which are critical for their journey through life.

Breaking the cycle of emotional immaturity is not an overnight endeavor. It requires patience, dedication, and a willingness to confront and heal from one's past. But the rewards are immeasurable. Not only do you give your children the gift of a nurturing, emotionally intelligent upbringing, but you also heal yourself in the process. As you embark on this path, remember that you are not alone. Support is available through friends, family, or professionals who can guide you along this transformative journey.

As we move forward, we will explore the principles of emotionally intelligent parenting in greater depth. By embracing these principles, you can ensure your children grow up with the emotional skills and resilience they need to thrive in an ever-changing world.

Emotionally Intelligent Parenting

Let's now shift our focus to the cultivation of emotional intelligence within parenting. Emotionally intelligent parenting is not merely a set of actions but a transformation of being, a conscious choice to foster an environment where emotional growth is as valued as intellectual and physical development.

Emotionally intelligent parenting begins with self-awareness. As a parent, recognizing your emotional state is crucial. It's about understanding your triggers, your strengths, and your limitations. This self-knowledge is the bedrock upon which you can build a stable and nurturing environment for your children. When you are aware of your emotional landscape, you can prevent immaturity from spilling over into your parenting style.

Communication is the next pillar of emotionally intelligent parenting. It involves listening with empathy and responding with clarity. Children raised by emotionally intelligent parents feel heard and understood. They are allowed to express their emotions without fear of judgment or dismissal. This open line of communication fosters trust and strengthens the parent-child bond.

Emotional regulation is another critical component. Parents who can manage their emotions model their children to do the same. It's not about suppressing feelings but about expressing them healthily and constructively. When children witness their parents navigating emotions gracefully, they learn to handle their emotional experiences with similar finesse.

Consistency in emotional responses is also vital. Children thrive on predictability, and when parents are consistent in their emotional reactions, it creates a sense of security. This doesn't mean you won't have bad days or moments of frustration. Still, it's about striving to handle these moments with a consistent approach that doesn't leave children feeling unstable or confused.

Finally, fostering empathy in your children is a gift that will serve them throughout their lives. By showing empathy to your children and others, you teach them to do the same. Empathy allows children to connect with others deeply emotionally, leading to more meaningful relationships and a greater understanding of the world around them.

Emotionally intelligent parenting is not an endpoint but a journey. It requires patience, dedication, and a willingness to grow alongside your children. By embracing these principles, you can give your children the tools they need to navigate the complexities of their emotions and the world. In doing so, you are raising emotionally healthy children and healing any remnants of emotional immaturity that may have been passed down through generations.

The Importance of Role Modeling

Role modeling is a beacon of transformation in redefining parenthood, especially after experiencing emotional immaturity from one's parents. Through our daily actions, responses, and decisions, children learn the most about navigating life's complexities. The silent lessons imparted by a parent's behavior often speak louder than any words of wisdom that might be shared around the dinner table.

Role modeling is not about striving for perfection but embracing authenticity and a willingness to grow. When parents exhibit the courage to acknowledge their emotions, manage them responsibly, and communicate effectively, they set a powerful example for their children. This demonstration of emotional intelligence lays the groundwork for children to develop their emotional maturity.

Consider the everyday scenarios where role modeling can have a profound impact. When a parent faces a setback at work and discusses the situation at home, they teach resilience, not with despair or avoidance but with a reflective and proactive attitude. When a parent apologizes after a moment of impatience, they teach accountability and the value of repairing relationships.

It is also in the quiet moments that role modeling takes shape. How a parent treats themselves with kindness and self-care teaches children about self-worth and the importance of personal well-being. The way parents interact with others, showing empathy and respect, even in challenging situations, offers a live demonstration of social skills that books and lectures alone cannot convey.

Moreover, role modeling extends beyond the emotional realm. It encompasses the values and ethics parents wish to instill in their children. By living these values, parents make them tangible for their children. Children are more likely to internalize these qualities, whether honesty, diligence, generosity or any other virtue when they see them in action.

In overcoming emotional immaturity, role modeling becomes even more significant. It is an opportunity to break dysfunction cycles and chart a new course for family dynamics. Parents who consciously model healthy emotional behaviors provide their children with a blueprint for emotional competence. This, in turn, can foster an environment where children feel safe to express themselves, learn from their experiences, and build strong, nurturing relationships.

Embracing the role of a model for emotional maturity is challenging. It requires introspection, a commitment to personal growth, and the humility to recognize that, as parents, we are also lifelong learners. Yet, the rewards of this endeavor are immeasurable. Through our example, we can empower our children to lead emotionally rich and fulfilling lives, equipped with the tools to navigate their relationships and personal challenges gracefully and confidently.

As we explore the facets of parenting after emotional immaturity, it becomes clear that the environment we create for our children is as crucial as the example we set. Within a nurturing environment, the seeds of emotional intelligence, sown by role modeling, can flourish.

Creating a Nurturing Environment

Creating a nurturing environment is one of the most pivotal steps in the parenting journey after emotional immaturity. This environment is not just a physical space but an emotional sanctuary that fosters growth, understanding, and connection. It is where children feel safe to express themselves, explore their identities, and develop resilience against life's adversities.

To cultivate such an environment, it is essential to establish clear and consistent boundaries. Boundaries are not barriers; they are the framework within which children can safely navigate their world. They provide a sense of security and predictability, essential for children who may have experienced the confusion and unpredictability of emotionally immature parenting. Communicating boundaries with kindness and clarity is crucial, ensuring they are age-appropriate and flexible enough to adapt to the child's growing needs.

Active listening plays a vital role in creating a nurturing environment. It involves giving full attention to the child, acknowledging their feelings without judgment, and validating their experiences. When children feel heard, they develop trust and are likelier to approach their parents for guidance and support. This practice also models for children how to listen to others, fostering empathy and social skills.

Emotional availability is another cornerstone of a nurturing environment. Being emotionally available means being present and responsive to a child's emotional needs. It requires parents to be attuned to their emotional states and to manage them effectively to be the steady presence their children need. This does not mean that parents must be perfect; instead, it is about being genuine and willing to own up to and learn from mistakes. This transparency can help children understand that it is okay to be imperfect and that growth is always possible.

Encouraging play and creativity is also essential. Play is children's language and a powerful tool for learning and expression. It allows children to explore different scenarios, practice problem-solving, and express their emotions in a safe context. Creative activities such as drawing, music, and storytelling can be therapeutic and help children process their feelings nonverbally.

Lastly, nurturing an environment of growth also means fostering independence. This involves encouraging children to make choices, take on age-appropriate responsibilities, and learn from the natural consequences of their actions. It is about guiding rather than controlling, allowing children to develop a sense of self-efficacy and confidence in their abilities.

Creating a nurturing environment is an ongoing process that requires patience, reflection, and a willingness to grow alongside your children. It is about building a foundation of love, respect, and understanding to support them throughout their lives. As parents work to provide this nurturing space, they heal the wounds of their past and lay the groundwork for their children's future well-being.

Support Systems and Resources

In redefining one's parenting after experiencing emotional immaturity from one's parents, it is essential to recognize that no individual is an island. The path to becoming a nurturing and emotionally attuned parent is often paved with the support of others. This support can come from various sources, each offering unique assistance and encouragement.

One of the most valuable resources for those seeking to break the cycle of emotional immaturity is therapy or counseling. A qualified mental health professional can provide a safe space to explore one's childhood experiences, understand their impact, and develop strategies for emotional growth. Therapists who specialize in family dynamics and intergenerational trauma can be particularly helpful, as they are equipped to address the specific challenges that come with this territory.

Support groups are another resource that can be immensely beneficial. Connecting with others who have had similar experiences can reduce isolation and provide a sense of community. Within these groups, individuals can share their struggles and successes, offering and receiving advice on navigating the complexities of parenting after emotional immaturity. These groups may exist within local communities or online, providing flexibility and accessibility to those in need.

Educational resources also play a critical role in the healing and growth process. Books, workshops, and seminars focusing on emotional intelligence, parenting skills, and personal development can offer insights and tools not instinctively known to someone who grew up with emotionally immature parents. Learning about healthy parent-child dynamics and effective communication techniques can empower individuals to create the nurturing environment they strive for in their families.

It is also important to cultivate personal relationships that foster growth and healing. Friends, family members, or mentors who understand and support one's journey can provide emotional sustenance. These relationships can offer practical help, such as childcare or advice, as well as emotional support, like validation and encouragement. Having at least one person who believes in one's ability to change and grow can make a significant difference.

Professional resources such as child psychologists or family therapists can be invaluable for parents looking to provide their children with the emotional support they may not have received. These professionals can assist in identifying the emotional needs of children and offer guidance on how to meet those needs effectively.

Lastly, self-care should be noticed as a resource. Parenting is a demanding task, and it is even more challenging for those working to heal their emotional wounds and taking time for themselves through meditation, exercise, or quiet reflection. Self-care ensures one has the emotional and physical energy to be present and responsive to their children's needs.

In summary, while the legacy of emotional immaturity from one's parents can be a heavy burden, there is a wealth of support systems and resources available to help lift that weight. By seeking out and utilizing these resources, individuals can heal themselves and provide their children with the emotionally rich upbringing they deserve.

Chapter Summary

- Breaking the cycle of emotional immaturity in parenting requires developing emotional intelligence, including empathy, emotional regulation, and secure attachments.
- Self-reflection on one's emotional past and learning emotional regulation strategies are critical steps toward intentional and responsive parenting.
- Empathy towards children's feelings and creating secure attachments are crucial for their emotional development and self-esteem.
- Emotionally intelligent parenting involves self-awareness, effective communication, and consistency in emotional responses to foster trust and security.
- Role modeling healthy emotional behaviors is essential for teaching children emotional maturity and resilience.
- A nurturing environment for children includes clear boundaries, active listening, emotional availability, encouragement of play and creativity, and fostering independence.
- Support systems such as therapy, support groups, educational resources, and personal relationships are vital for parents overcoming emotional immaturity.
- Self-care is an essential resource for parents, ensuring they have the emotional and physical energy to be present and responsive to their children's needs.

10

SOCIETAL IMPLICATIONS AND MOVING FORWARD

The Broader Impact of Emotional Immaturity

Emotional immaturity in parents is not an isolated phenomenon, nor does it solely affect the immediate family dynamics. Its ripples extend far beyond the confines of the home, touching upon various facets of society in subtle yet profound ways. The broader impact of such emotional immaturity can be observed in educational systems, workplaces, and even in the broader cultural narratives that shape our understanding of parenting and personal development.

In educational settings, teachers and counselors often encounter the indirect consequences of emotionally immature parenting. Children from such backgrounds may exhibit a range of behaviors, from heightened anxiety and difficulty with peer relationships to challenges with authority and a lack of self-regulation. These behaviors can disrupt classrooms and require additional resources and attention, impacting not only the child in question but also their peers and educators.

Within the workplace, adults who grew up with emotionally immature parents might struggle with professional relationships and self-esteem. They may struggle to navigate constructive criticism, manage stress effectively, or assert themselves healthily. These difficulties can lead to a less cohesive work environment. They may even affect the overall productivity and well-being of employees.

On a societal level, emotionally immature parenting perpetuates a cycle of emotional dysfunction that can hinder the development of emotional intelligence—a key component in fostering a compassionate and progressive society. When emotional immaturity is modeled and normalized, it becomes more difficult for subsequent generations to develop the emotional skills necessary to build strong, resilient communities.

Furthermore, the media often portrays parenting in a way that either idealizes or vilifies the role, with little attention given to the nuanced reality of raising children. This can create unrealistic expectations and perpetuate stigma, making it harder for parents to seek help or for children to understand and address their experiences.

The cost of emotional immaturity in parents is not just a personal or familial issue; it is also an economic one. Mental health services, social support programs, and educational interventions require significant investment, and the lack of emotional skills can lead to increased reliance on such services. By addressing the problem's root—helping parents develop emotional maturity—we can reduce the long-term financial burden on these systems.

As we move forward, it is essential to recognize the pervasive nature of this issue and the importance of addressing it not just in homes but as a collective societal challenge. By changing the narrative around emotional maturity, we can begin to break the cycle and lay the groundwork for healthier, more emotionally intelligent future generations. This involves creating spaces for open dialogue, providing resources for parents and children alike, and reshaping cultural expectations to value emotional growth as a lifelong journey.

Changing the Narrative

In the fabric of our society, the stories we tell ourselves about parenting and emotional maturity are deeply woven into the collective consciousness. Cultural norms, societal expectations, and generational beliefs have historically shaped these narratives. However, as we become more aware of the complexities of human psychology and the pivotal role of emotional development, it is time for us to reexamine and reshape these stories for the betterment of future generations.

Emotionally immature parents, often through no fault of their own, may have been raised in environments where emotional expression was discouraged or even punished. This cycle of emotional suppression is perpetuated when these individuals, in turn, become parents themselves, lacking the tools to foster emotional intelligence in their children. The narrative has long been that parents are infallible figures of authority. Still, this view does not account for the human element of parenting—the vulnerabilities, the uncertainties, and the capacity for growth.

Changing the narrative means acknowledging that emotional immaturity is not a static trait but a dynamic one that can be addressed and improved upon with awareness and effort. It means recognizing that parents, like their children, are on a journey of emotional development that may require support, education, and sometimes, intervention.

To move forward, we must cultivate a culture that values emotional intelligence as a critical parenting component. This involves creating spaces for open dialogue about the emotional challenges of parenthood without judgment or stigma. It means providing resources for parents to learn about emotional regulation, empathy, and healthy communication. By doing so, we can empower parents to break the cycle of emotional immaturity, offering them the opportunity to grow alongside their children.

Moreover, changing the narrative also involves acknowledging the resilience and strength of those who have grown up with emotionally immature parents. Many have had to navigate their emotional landscapes mainly independently, often becoming self-reliant and empathetic adults. Their stories are tales of struggle, profound personal development, and triumph. By honoring these journeys, we validate their experiences and provide hope and inspiration for others in similar situations.

In this reimagining of our societal story, we must also address the systemic barriers that prevent individuals from accessing the support they need. Economic disparities, social inequalities, and cultural differences can all impact a person's ability to seek help in developing emotional maturity. By advocating for inclusive, accessible mental health services and educational programs, we can begin to dismantle these barriers and create a more emotionally intelligent society.

As we endeavor to change the narrative, we must remember that this is not a task for the few but a mission for the many. It requires the collective efforts of educators, mental health professionals, policymakers, and communities to shift perceptions and create lasting change. Through this collaborative spirit, we can rewrite the story of parenting, one where emotional maturity is not just an aspiration but a reality for all.

Advocacy and Awareness

In the wake of recognizing the pervasive influence of emotionally immature parents on both individual lives and society at large, it becomes imperative to foster a culture of advocacy and awareness. The journey towards healing and societal change is not solitary; it requires collective acknowledgment and action.

Advocacy for the issues stemming from emotionally immature parenting begins with giving a voice to those affected. Many adults carry the invisible scars of their childhood experiences, often without realizing the source of their struggles. By creating platforms where these stories can be shared, we validate individual experiences and illuminate the common patterns that emerge in the lives of emotionally immature parents. This collective storytelling can break the silence surrounding this topic, encouraging others to come forward and seek the support they need.

Awareness, on the other hand, is a broader societal endeavor. It involves educating the public about the characteristics and consequences of emotional immaturity in parents. Awareness campaigns can take many forms, from public service announcements to social media campaigns, each designed to inform and enlighten the general populace. The goal is to shift the cultural perception, making it widely known that emotional immaturity is not a personal failing of the child but a behavioral pattern of the parent that can be addressed and improved upon.

Moreover, advocacy and awareness go hand in hand with professional development. Mental health professionals, educators, and social workers need to be equipped with the tools to recognize the signs of emotional immaturity in parents and support the children and adults affected by it. Training programs and continuing education courses can be instrumental in spreading this knowledge, ensuring that those in helping professions are prepared to intervene effectively and compassionately.

In the realm of policy, advocacy can lead to the development of support systems and legal frameworks that protect and assist children and families dealing with the impacts of emotionally immature parenting. This could include the implementation of parenting programs that emphasize emotional intelligence and resilience, as well as the provision of resources for children and adults seeking to heal from their childhood experiences.

The path forward is one of proactive engagement and empathy. By advocating for understanding and awareness, we can begin to dismantle the stigma associated with the repercussions of being raised by emotionally immature parents. Through these concerted efforts, we hope to see a future where emotional maturity is not just a personal virtue but a societal norm, where families can thrive in an environment of emotional health and well-being.

Educational Initiatives

Now, we must recognize the pivotal role of education. Educational initiatives provide the bedrock for equipping individuals with the knowledge and skills necessary to foster emotional maturity in personal and communal contexts.

The essence of such initiatives is not merely the transmission of information but the cultivation of environments where emotional intelligence is valued and nurtured. To this end, schools and educational institutions can play a transformative role. By integrating emotional literacy into curricula, educators can provide students with the tools to understand and manage their emotions and recognize and respond to the emotional needs of others.

One of the foundational steps in this educational endeavor is incorporating social and emotional learning (SEL) programs. These programs are designed to teach children from a young age about self-awareness, self-management, social awareness, relationship skills, and responsible decision-making. By embedding these competencies into the education fabric, children can develop a more nuanced understanding of their emotional landscape and that of others.

Furthermore, parent education programs are essential in breaking the cycle of emotional immaturity. These programs allow parents and caregivers to learn about healthy emotional development, effective communication strategies, and ways to build strong, empathetic relationships with their children. Providing support and resources can empower parents to model emotional maturity, setting a positive example for the next generation.

In addition to formal education settings, community-based workshops and online resources can extend the reach of these teachings. Public seminars and digital platforms can offer adults access to further their understanding of emotional maturity. Through these channels, the principles of emotional intelligence can permeate various aspects of society, from the workplace to family life.

Moreover, professional development for educators and mental health professionals is crucial. Training programs that emphasize the importance of emotional maturity can enhance the ability of these professionals to support not only the children in their care but also the parents who may struggle with their emotional growth.

In fostering educational initiatives that prioritize emotional maturity, we are investing in the well-being of our communities. By equipping individuals with the understanding and skills to navigate the complexities of emotional interactions, we lay the groundwork for healthier relationships and a more compassionate society. As we move forward, it is our collective responsibility to ensure that these educational efforts are inclusive, comprehensive, and reflective of the diverse needs of our communities.

Building Emotionally Mature Communities

In the quest to nurture emotionally mature communities, we must look beyond the confines of formal education and consider the broader tapestry of societal influences that shape our emotional development. The family unit, often the first social structure we encounter, plays a pivotal role. When parents are emotionally immature, they may inadvertently instill similar patterns in their children, perpetuating a cycle that can ripple through communities.

To break this cycle, we must foster environments that encourage emotional growth, not just in children but in adults as well. This calls for a cultural shift that values emotional intelligence alongside academic and professional achievements. We can begin by creating community programs offering support and resources for parents who want to develop their emotional maturity. These include workshops on effective communication, empathy, emotional regulation, and support groups where parents can share experiences and strategies.

Moreover, we must recognize that emotional maturity is not a destination but a journey. Communities can benefit from promoting lifelong learning in the emotional realm. Just as we might attend a gym to maintain physical health, we could benefit from regular 'emotional fitness' sessions to enhance our emotional well-being. These could be public lectures, meditation groups, or art and music therapy sessions designed to cultivate self-awareness, compassion, and resilience.

In addition, local governments and organizations can play a crucial role by integrating emotional maturity into their policies and practices. This might involve training community leaders and public servants in emotional intelligence, ensuring they can lead by example and make decisions considering the emotional well-being of the populations they serve.

It is also essential to provide accessible mental health services within communities. By removing the stigma around seeking help and making it easy and affordable to access therapists and counselors, we can encourage individuals to work on their emotional issues before they impact their parenting or other areas of community life.

Finally, the media and entertainment industries have a powerful influence on societal norms and values. By promoting narratives that showcase emotionally mature behavior, these industries can help shift public perception and inspire individuals to aspire to more incredible emotional growth.

Building emotionally mature communities requires a collective effort and a willingness to invest in the emotional health of all members. It is a process that will take time to happen. Still, with dedication and compassion, we can create a society where emotional intelligence is cherished and nurtured, allowing future generations to thrive in a more understanding, empathetic, and emotionally aware world.

Chapter Summary

- Emotional immaturity in parents affects society, including education, workplaces, and cultural narratives about parenting.
- In schools, children of emotionally immature parents may struggle with anxiety, peer relationships, and authority, impacting the learning environment.
- Adults from such backgrounds may face professional relationships and self-esteem difficulties, affecting workplace cohesion and productivity.

- Emotionally immature parenting perpetuates cycles of emotional dysfunction, hindering societal emotional intelligence and resilience.
- Media portrayals of parenting often lack nuance, creating unrealistic expectations and stigmatizing struggles, making it harder to seek help.
- The economic cost of emotional immaturity is significant, with increased reliance on mental health services and social support programs.
- Changing societal narratives around emotional maturity involves acknowledging parents' emotional growth journeys and providing support.
- Advocacy and awareness are crucial for addressing the impact of emotionally immature parenting, requiring collective action and policy changes.

EMBRACING EMOTIONAL MATURITY

Personal Reflections

As we draw near to the close of this exploration into the world shaped by emotionally immature parents, I find myself pausing to reflect on the personal journeys that have intersected with the pages of this book. Each story shared and each insight gained has illuminated the challenges faced and cast a hopeful light on the path to emotional maturity.

In the quiet moments of introspection, I am reminded that understanding emotional immaturity is not just an academic pursuit. It is deeply personal. For many, it resonates with the echoes of childhood experiences, the struggles of navigating relationships, and the arduous journey toward self-awareness and healing. The courage displayed by those who have shared their stories with me, and by extension with you, the reader, is nothing short of inspirational. Their vulnerability has opened the door to a collective healing process that extends beyond the individual to touch the lives of others.

It is in these personal reflections that we find the seeds of change. Recognizing the traits of emotional immaturity in our parents is not an end but a beginning. It is the first step in a transformative process that allows us to break free from the cycles of the past. By acknowledging the pain, the confusion, and the longing for what might have been, we permit ourselves to seek a different narrative for our lives.

The journey towards emotional maturity is not a solitary one. It is a path we walk together, learning from each other's experiences and supporting our growth. As we embrace the complexities of our emotions, we learn to navigate them with grace and understanding. We learn that to be emotionally mature is not to be devoid of emotion but to engage with our feelings healthily and constructively.

This personal growth has a profound impact on how we raise our children, how we interact with our peers, and how we contribute to society. By striving for emotional maturity, we set a new standard for ourselves and those who seek guidance. We become beacons of stability and empathy, capable of nurturing relationships built on mutual respect and genuine connection.

As we move forward, let us carry the lessons learned and shared wisdom. Let us be gentle with ourselves as we navigate the complexities of our emotional landscapes. And remember that every step taken towards emotional maturity is a step towards a more compassionate and understanding world.

In the next section, we will explore how these personal transformations can ripple outward, creating waves of change that reach far beyond our immediate circles. The journey continues, and we contribute to a legacy of emotional health and resilience for generations with each step.

The Ripple Effect of Change

It is essential to recognize the profound influence our transformation can have on the world around us. This change, although deeply personal, does not occur in isolation. It sends out ripples that touch the lives of others, often in ways we cannot foresee.

The path to emotional maturity is marked by increased self-awareness, empathy, and the ability to foster healthy relationships. As individuals break the cycle of emotional immaturity, they become role models for others. Friends, siblings, and acquaintances may witness this evolution and find inspiration to embark on their journeys of self-discovery and healing.

Moreover, the shift towards emotional maturity within a family can have a transformative effect on its dynamics. Children who grow up with parents committed to their emotional development benefit from a stable and nurturing environment. This foundation equips them with the emotional intelligence and resilience necessary to navigate life's challenges more effectively.

In the broader context of society, embracing emotional maturity contributes to creating communities that value emotional intelligence and mental well-being. Workplaces can become more compassionate and supportive; schools can implement programs that prioritize the emotional development of students, and social policies can be crafted with a deeper understanding of the human psyche.

The ripple effect of change also extends to the cultural narrative around parenting and emotional health. As more individuals speak openly about their experiences and the importance of emotional maturity, there is a gradual shift in societal expectations and norms. This openness paves the way for future generations to approach parenting and personal development with greater awareness and intentionality.

Ultimately, the journey toward emotional maturity is not just about healing from the past; it's about creating a legacy of emotional health that will benefit future generations. It is a testament to the human spirit's capacity for growth and the enduring impact that one person's transformation can have on the fabric of society.

Hope for Future Generations

As we draw the curtains on our exploration of emotionally immature parents, we find ourselves standing at the threshold of a new era. In this era, the seeds of emotional maturity can be sown for the benefit of future generations. The journey through understanding the complexities of emotional immaturity in parents has been arduous yet enlightening, and it is with a heart full of hope that we look forward to the possibilities that lie ahead.

Hope, as a beacon, shines brightest in the aftermath of struggle. The awareness and insights gained from the preceding chapters will empower individuals to break the cycles of emotional immaturity that have, for too long, been passed down through generations. This hope is not a passive wish but a call to action—to embrace the responsibility of nurturing emotional growth within ourselves and our communities.

The prospect of raising emotionally mature generations begins with the individual. It starts with the conscious decision to embark on a journey of self-reflection and healing. For those who have experienced the challenges of having emotionally immature parents, this may mean seeking support, engaging in therapy, or finding solace in communities that understand their plight. It is through these personal transformations that the foundation for change is built.

Moreover, the hope for future generations is fortified by knowing that emotional maturity can be learned and cultivated. Parents, educators, and caregivers who understand emotional development can actively foster environments where children are encouraged to express their feelings, develop empathy, and build resilience. By modeling emotional maturity—expressing emotions healthily, setting boundaries, and practicing self-care—adults can provide invaluable lessons that children carry into adulthood.

The ripple effect of these individual changes is profound. As more people embrace emotional maturity, societal norms begin to shift. What was once a culture that may have inadvertently perpetuated emotional immaturity becomes one that values emotional intelligence and psychological well-being. This cultural shift can transform relationships, workplaces, and communities, leading to a more compassionate and empathetic world.

In this hopeful future, the legacy of emotional maturity is not just the absence of the negative traits associated with emotional immaturity but positive, nurturing relationships supporting the individual's holistic development. It is a future where emotional maturity is not an exception but a norm—a cherished value passed on with intention and care.

As we stand on the cusp of this hopeful horizon, we recognize that the journey does not end here. The conversation about emotional maturity is ongoing, and it is through continued dialogue and education that progress is made. Each step taken towards emotional maturity, no matter how small, is a step towards a brighter, more emotionally intelligent future for all generations.

Continuing the Conversation

As we draw near the conclusion of this journey, it is essential to recognize that the dialogue surrounding emotionally immature parents does not end with the turning of the last page. Much like the process of personal growth and healing, the conversation is ongoing. It is a continuous exchange of experiences, insights, and support that extends beyond the confines of this book and into the living fabric of our daily lives.

Embracing emotional maturity is not a destination but a path we walk daily. It is a commitment to self-awareness, empathy, and the willingness to engage in the sometimes challenging process of personal development. For those who have grown up with emotionally immature parents, this path can be particularly arduous, as it often involves unlearning patterns and beliefs that have been deeply ingrained since childhood.

Yet, it is within this very challenge that opportunity lies. Each step taken towards understanding and healing is a step away from the shadows of the past and towards a future of emotional resilience. By continuing to converse about these experiences, we validate our feelings and struggles and pave the way for others to find their voice and begin their journeys toward healing.

The conversation can take many forms. It may be found in support groups and therapy sessions, in the quiet confidences shared between friends, or even in the stories we tell ourselves about who we are and aspire to be. In these exchanges, we find the strength to confront our vulnerabilities and the courage to challenge the legacies of emotional immaturity.

Remember, you are not alone in this. The shared narratives of those who have navigated similar waters are a beacon of hope and a testament to the human capacity for growth and change. By continuing the conversation, we foster a community that upholds emotional maturity as a valued ideal that is attainable and worth striving for.

As we move forward, let us carry with us the understanding that our past does not have to dictate our future. We have the power to redefine our relationships, set boundaries, and cultivate the emotional health we may have felt was missing in our formative years. In doing so, we heal ourselves and break the cycle, offering hope for future generations to live with greater emotional intelligence and connectedness.

The dialogue about emotionally immature parents is evolving, with each of us contributing to its depth and richness. Continuing the conversation ensures that this vital topic remains in the light, where it can be examined, understood, and transcended.

Final Words of Encouragement

As we draw the curtains on our exploration of emotionally immature parents and the journey toward emotional maturity, I hope that you have found solace, understanding, and a path forward within these pages. The road to healing and growth is seldom straight or free of obstacles, but it is a road that leads to a more prosperous, more fulfilling life.

If you have recognized the shadows of emotional immaturity in your upbringing, know that the awareness you now hold is a decisive first step. The light can guide you through the process of untangling the complex emotions and patterns woven into your life's fabric. It is okay to feel many emotions—anger, sadness, compassion, or relief. These feelings are valid and signposts on your emotional maturity journey.

Embracing emotional maturity is about understanding where we come from and where we choose to go. It is about making conscious choices that align with our values and sense of self. It is about setting boundaries with kindness and assertiveness and nurturing reciprocal and respectful relationships. Remember, emotional maturity is not a destination but a continual growth, learning, and self-reflection process.

As you move forward, carry the knowledge that you are not alone. Many have walked this path before you, and many will walk it after. There is strength in the shared human experience and power in the stories we tell. With all its complexity and nuance, your story is an integral part of this tapestry.

Take heart in that every step you take toward emotional maturity is a step toward a more authentic life. It is a courageous act to break the cycle of emotional immaturity that requires patience and self-compassion. Be gentle with yourself as you navigate this path, and remember to celebrate the small victories along the way.

In closing, I encourage you to hold onto hope. Hope for the relationships that can be healed, the personal growth that awaits, and the generational changes your emotional maturity can inspire. Your journey may inspire others to embark on their own, creating ripples of positive change that extend far beyond what you imagine.

Thank you for allowing me to be a part of your journey. May you move forward with a heart full of courage, a mind open to learning, and a spirit ready to embrace the beauty of emotional maturity.

Your Feedback Matters

As we reach the end of this book, I extend my heartfelt gratitude for your time and engagement. It's been an honor to share this journey with you, and I hope it has been as enriching for you as it has been for me.

If the ideas we've explored have sparked new thoughts, inspired change, or provided comfort, I'd really appreciate it if you could share your experience with others. Your feedback benefits me as an author and guides fellow readers in their quest for their next meaningful read.

To leave a review on Amazon, follow the QR code below. Your insights and reflections are invaluable; by sharing them, you contribute to a larger conversation that extends far beyond the pages of this book.

Thank you once again for your company on this literary adventure. May the insights you've gained stay with you, and may your continuous quest for knowledge be ever-fulfilling.

ABOUT THE AUTHOR

Essie Woodard is an author best known for her groundbreaking book series "Generational Healing." With a background in psychology and a passion for helping individuals break free from the chains of their past, Woodard has dedicated her career to exploring the complex realms of inherited family trauma and the challenges of dealing with emotionally immature parents. Her work offers insightful analysis, practical personal growth, and healing strategies, resonating with readers worldwide.

Made in the USA
Las Vegas, NV
29 February 2024